William Robertson

The Martyrs of Blantyre

Henry Henderson, Dr. John Bowie and Robert Cleland - a chapter from the story of missions in central Africa. Second Edition

William Robertson

The Martyrs of Blantyre
Henry Henderson, Dr. John Bowie and Robert Cleland - a chapter from the story of missions in central Africa. Second Edition

ISBN/EAN: 9783337243722

Printed in Europe, USA, Canada, Australia, Japan

Cover: Foto ©ninafisch / pixelio.de

More available books at **www.hansebooks.com**

THE MARTYRS OF BLANTYRE

HENDERSON—BOWIE—CLELAND

Frontispiece. BLANTYRE CHURCH, EAST AFRICA.

THE
MARTYRS OF BLANTYRE

HENRY HENDERSON
DR. JOHN BOWIE
ROBERT CLELAND

A CHAPTER FROM THE STORY OF MISSIONS

IN

CENTRAL AFRICA

BY THE

REV. WILLIAM ROBERTSON, M.A.
CHURCH OF SCOTLAND DEPUTY FOR HOME MISSIONS

Second Edition

LONDON
JAMES NISBET & CO., 21 BERNERS STREET
MDCCCXCII

TO

THE MISSIONARIES OF THE CHURCH OF SCOTLAND

IN

CENTRAL AFRICA

I DEDICATE

𝕿𝖍𝖎𝖘 𝕷𝖎𝖙𝖙𝖑𝖊 𝕭𝖔𝖔𝖐

IN AFFECTIONATE REMEMBRANCE OF THEIR

FRIENDS AND MINE.

PREFACE.

This book is issued as a simple memorial of three devoted lives. Those whose story it tells were "Martyrs," not in the sense of having been slain for the truth, but in the no less real sense of being Witnesses for the testimony of Jesus Christ, who, with unswerving courage and devotion, laid down their lives in the African mission-field. The aim of the book is to give, in a short simple sketch, such a glimpse of them and their work as will convey to the reader some idea of what manner of men they were and what kind of work they did for Africa. It is not in any sense a complete biography of any of them, nor does it touch at all on questions of either Mission or State policy. Every effort has been made, however, to secure that it should be reliable, and all the information contained in it accurate and up to date.

If it should be the means of helping any one to a clearer appreciation of what life in the African mission-field is, or of begetting in any heart a deeper sympathy with those who are labouring there, it will have served its purpose.

I desire to record my thanks to the many friends, both here and in Africa, to whose kindness I have been indebted for help in its preparation and for the perusal of letters and other sources of information, Acknowledgment is also due to the representatives of *The Mission Record* and the *Foreign Mission Committee* for the facilities and assistance which they have cordially afforded me.

May God use the story of those who now rest from their labours to inspire others to a like faith with theirs.

EDINBURGH. *February* 1892.

CONTENTS.

		PAGE
I.	INTRODUCTION	11
II.	THE PRAYER OF THE DEAD LIVINGSTONE AND ITS ANSWER	17
III.	BLANTYRE	35
IV.	HENRY HENDERSON, THE PIONEER	53
V.	DR. JOHN BOWIE, MEDICAL MISSIONARY	75
VI.	ROBERT CLELAND, THE MISSIONARY OF MILANJE	103
VII.	CONCLUSION	139

APPENDIX—

    I. STAFF OF THE BLANTYRE MISSION . . 147

    II. MINUTE OF GENERAL ASSEMBLY ON THE DEATHS OF MISSIONARIES AT BLANTYRE . . . 148

ILLUSTRATIONS.

New Church, Blantyre . . .	*Frontispiece*
An African Home . .	. *Page* 39
Manganja and Yao . .	,, 50
Portraits of Mr. and Mrs. Henderson	. ,, 55
Portrait of Dr. Bowie .	,, 77
Portrait of the Rev. Robert Cleland	,. 105
Chart of Shiré Highlands showing the Mission Stations of the Church of Scotland, by the Rev. A. Hetherwick, F.R.G.S.	*at end*

I.

Introduction.

I.

INTRODUCTION.

THE eyes of the world are on Africa at present. One cannot take up a newspaper without finding the Dark Continent, in one or other of its great regions, —Northern, Southern, Central,—claiming attention by the doings of the explorer, the soldier, the politician, or the missionary. Every now and again a quiver of interest thrills through the Cabinets of Europe at the surgings to and fro in the great scramble for Africa; while, on the other hand, the inrush of European life —English, German, Portuguese—with its diverse influences, and the formation of great chartered companies, all eager to colonise, to claim, to annex, is stirring the stagnant pool of African life. The evolutions are rapid, and almost before the world has had time to take in the situation which one ferment has produced the state of things has changed and another has begun. Struggle and death, prospect and progress, initial defeat and final triumph, follow each other in rapid succession. The expectation of yesterday is realised to-day and to-morrow is left behind. The map of Africa is changing so quickly that the geographer has a hard time keeping it up to date, and the public can hardly find leisure to make and keep themselves familiar with it.

In that swift rush the changes are so many and the events so important, that we are apt to lose sight of the men whose courage and devotion are achieving these results. Once in a while a Stanley, a Gordon, or a Hannington rivets public attention for a moment and becomes known to the world. But of the large number of devoted men and women whose life and labours have gone to the making of Africa, only a very few are, to most people, anything more than mere names. Yet never to have had even if it were but a glimpse of such lives is to miss a great deal that helps one to understand Africa and the problems it presents.

This is emphatically true of those who have laboured and died in the mission-field, and nowhere is it more strikingly true than in that part of Central Africa opened up by the explorations of Livingstone, and which is now being won for Christianity by those who have followed in his footsteps. To know them and their work brings one into touch, not only with the progress of civilisation, but with the coming of the kingdom of God there.

Among the many followers of Livingstone the three whose story this little book tells were men that were "worth the knowing," and many considerations make it fitting that the three lives should be linked together.

They were all Scotchmen. They were all sons of the University of Edinburgh. They were all in the service of the Church of Scotland's Mission at Blantyre, in the Shiré Hills, and so were intimate personal friends. One was a pioneer missionary, one a medical missionary, and one an ordained minister of Jesus Christ; but all three were men of the Livingstone type, unwavering in determination, unfailing in their faith in God, and unwearying in their devotion to Africa and their love for the African. A further and sad link of association is found in the fact that they fell almost together in swift succession. Although, by the goodness of God, the Blantyre Mission during its fifteen years of brave and trying work had never been called to mourn a man taken from its staff by death, yet within three short months (November 1890 to February 1891) these three —first Cleland, then Bowie, then Henderson—were each laid in an African grave; while Mrs. Henderson and their only child were also taken at the same time. It was a dark, sad time, and in its sorrowful remembrance the three names will be linked together. They did not fall by the spear or assegai of the savage, yet none the less truly did each of them, with a devotion which regarded not himself, lay down his life a witness for the Gospel of Jesus Christ. Each life had its own story, and it has been thought best to tell each by itself. It is believed, too, that the story of the lives will be more sympathetically read if their environment is understood; and therefore we give a short sketch of the great cause in which they enlisted,—the cause of Christian Missions in East Central Africa,—with a more particular account of the Mission at Blantyre, to the building up of which they gave their labours and their lives.

II.

The Prayer of the Dead Livingstone and its Answer.

II.

THE PRAYER OF THE DEAD LIVINGSTONE AND ITS ANSWER.

EVERY one remembers how, on May Day 1873, in a poor grass hut at Ilala, on the shores of Lake Bangweolo, the dead Livingstone was found kneeling by his bed in the attitude of prayer. In loneliness and weakness, wasted by sickness and weary with many wanderings, he had died as he had lived—praying,—and on the breath of that last prayer the weary spirit had gone home to God. It was a sight to touch men's hearts; but there, in the lonely African forest, there was no white man to look on it or to tell the world what it was. Only the dark African saw it, and though he bowed reverently before it, what was he that he should be able to catch the spirit of that scene or interpret it for the strange world without? Yet the silent prayer of those cold lips, the pathetic appeal of that pale face buried in the folded hands, spoke with a voice that would not be silent, and with a power that would not be repressed until it had not only reached the ear of God, but moved the hearts of men to the uttermost ends of the earth. Wave upon wave, in ever-widening circles, the voice of that prayer was borne till from all Christendom there came an answer to its cry. The cold lips were now dumb, but the prayer of the life spoke instead till men could not help but hear. That poor kneeling form seemed the very embodiment of all the prayers, the expression of all the labours of the devoted life which had been poured out, a sacrifice for Africa. It seemed to pour a spirit of burning fire into many a prayer that he had offered and many an appeal that he had made while he was here, till they came back and scorched the hearts that had been deaf to them before. "May the blessing of God rest," those lips had once said, and now the spent life seemed to echo it—"May the blessing of God rest on the man, be he Englishman or American or Turk, who will heal this open sore of the world." "I have opened the door," the living voice had said to the students at Cambridge, and now the voice of the dead seemed to repeat it—"I have opened the door: see that you let no man shut it!"

How the cry of that finished life was borne from land to land! First the dark Makololo heard it as they looked into the empty hut, and it caught them like a spell. Under its influence they tenderly lifted the body of their dead leader and bore it through countless miles of forest to the sea-coast, and thence across the sea, till they saw it laid with the honoured dead of his own land. But they did more, else the voice of the dead had lost half its power. They gathered together with affectionate carefulness all those note-books and papers of which he had taken such care, and at which they had so often seen him writing laboriously when head and hand were alike weary; and with such scrupulous care did they carry them to England that, when they were opened and examined, it was found that the papers presented a continuous narrative of seven years' exploration and experience *without a single break*,—not one entry being lost or one word destroyed! One hardly knows whether most to admire the faithfulness or to marvel at the feat. Surely God had designed that the appeal of the dead Livingstone should not be silenced, even by death in the solitude of the African forest.

Then Europe and America heard, and stood still a moment to listen, as to a cry for help. That cry awoke in the heart of civilization feelings of indignant shame that the horrible trade in human flesh should be allowed to continue after Livingstone had shown it up and died to destroy it. Once awakened, civilization called for more light and fuller knowledge of "that unknown land," and time and again the explorer went forth to search its depths and bring back such knowledge of it as could be gathered. Stanley, Thomson, Cameron, Keith Johnstone, Wissmann, and other travellers followed each other in rapid succession, till by-and-by the world began to know something of the land and the people that were enshrined in the prayer of the dead Livingstone.

But,—most momentous of all,—that cry awoke the Church of God. At sound of it men caught the glow of the Livingstone spirit—that spirit which he had caught from a Greater than himself—and a desire arose to enter this land of suffering and blood, to cleanse it of its horrors and claim it and its people for the living Christ. As with one impulse, the hearts of men in different branches of the Christian Church were moved to send to its down-trodden races the glad tidings of salvation, liberty to the captives, and joy to the oppressed. In the words of Livingstone himself, "the end of the geographical feat was the beginning of missionary enterprise." The dreams of one period became the realities of the next. The vision that had cheered the weary steps of the great explorer began almost at once to be realised. He had tracked the path of the Arab caravan along the great slave-route from Zanzibar into the interior, and again up the great waterway of Central Africa by the Zambezi and the Shiré, through the Shiré Hills to Lake Shirwa, and over the tableland to Lake Nyasa, and everywhere along both routes he saw the slaver's trail. Everywhere he saw the villainous Arab march inland in quest of ivory, provoking war, burning villages, scattering slaughter and ruin among the natives, and then return with his capture of ivory and his gang of slaves, who had to drag their way through such unspeakable suffering and horrors that only one out of every ten of them ever reached the coast to be sold and shipped off, although a British Consul at Zanzibar has stated that no fewer than 19,000 slaves are exported annually from that part of Africa alone. It made him heart-sore to see, as he said, "strings of wretched slaves yoked together in their heavy slave-sticks, some carrying ivory, others copper, or food for the march; whilst hope and fear, misery and villainy, may be read off on the various faces that pass in line out of this country, like a serpent dragging its accursed folds away from the victim it has paralysed with its fangs." Then he prayed for a time when along that same route there would flow from a Christian world without, into the heart of that Dark Continent, thus cursed with sin and suffering, a stream of life bearing the light of God and the blessings of Christianity. He knew that that time would come, and that it could only come through a great uprising of missionary devotion, and he prayed for that. Now, when his eye was not there to see nor his hand to welcome it, the answer to his prayer came. As you have seen star after star break through the darkness of an autumn night, so did Mission after Mission appear shining out in that African darkness, each star a little world of life and love,—each a Bethlehem star telling by its light that the Redeemer had come. Entering from the east coast and moving up that great waterway which he himself had discovered, the rising tide of the new life began to flow, bearing on its bosom God's answer to his prayers.

The first to come was *The Universities' Mission*. Like

an evening star shining faintly before the sunset, it came before Livingstone had died, but it was the first-fruits of his labours. So far back as 1857 he had, when in England, addressed a crowded meeting of students at Cambridge, and in closing an impassioned appeal to them he said, "I go back to Africa to try to make an open path for commerce and Christianity. Do you carry out the work which I have begun. I LEAVE IT WITH YOU." The response to that appeal was the combination of the universities of England and Ireland for the formation and support of a *Universities' Mission* to Central Africa, and the despatch in October 1860 of a Mission party, under the direction of a Scotchman, Bishop Mackenzie, who was accompanied by two clergymen and the now famous Horace Waller, afterwards editor of Livingstone's last Journals—not then, however, in Holy Orders, but acting as a lay superintendent.

Their instructions being to establish a Mission "in the footsteps of Livingstone," the party settled at Magomero, near Lake Shirwa, among the Manganja people dwelling on the hills to the east of the River Shiré. The sad story of this Mission, its misfortunes, and the circumstances which led to its withdrawal after the death of Bishop Mackenzie, who died of fever at a place near the mouth of the Ruo, two hundred miles inland, have already been told. It had to retire from the Shiré region, transferring the sphere of its operations to Zanzibar, but it left behind it as one of *the landmarks* pointing the way, the grave of Bishop Mackenzie, with a rough iron cross which Livingstone afterwards planted over it, and the memory among the natives of a brave and good man, whom they remembered as "Muntu oa nkoma ntima"—*a man of a sweet heart*.

In more recent days the *Universities' Mission* has again worked its way, by a succession of mission-stations, from Zanzibar northward to Usambara on the one hand, and on the other along the line of the Rovuma westward to those Shiré Hills and Nyasaland, one of its most interesting and active stations being on Likoma Island in Lake Nyasa, a centre from which, by means of its missionary steamer, the *Charles Janson*, it carries the light to various places along the shore of the lake; while the repeated journeys of Bishop Smythies over the wide tract of country placed under his care, and the devoted labours of such men as Archdeacon Maples, the Rev. W. P. Johnson, and other members of the Mission staff, are fast kindling the light of God in the heart of that land of darkness.

But the early days of this Mission were before the Church had awakened at the news of Livingstone's death. When that came men's hearts were stirred, and his own countrymen especially felt that it would be shame indeed upon them if that opened door were now allowed to be closed. Accordingly, almost simultaneously there arose in all the Presbyterian Churches of Scotland a movement in favour of organising a missionary invasion of East Central Africa, with the Zambezi and Shiré as its route, and Lake Nyasa and the Shiré Highlands as the field of its conquest. The enterprise of the Free Church led the way; the Church of Scotland, inspired by the zeal of the late Dr. Macrae of Hawick, cordially joined; and the African experience of Dr. Stewart of Lovedale gave practical direction to the movement. A pioneer expedition composed of representatives of the different Churches, under the command of Mr. E. D. Young, R.N., was despatched in 1875, the representative of the Church of Scotland being Henry Henderson. The story of its experiences will be found in another chapter.

Out of this expedition two Missions grew. At Cape Maclear, on the shore of Lake Nyasa, is *Livingstonia*, one of the Missions of the Free Church of Scotland, in the working of which the United Presbyterian Church and the Reformed Dutch Church of South Africa also share. It was founded in 1876 by the Rev. Dr. Stewart of Lovedale, who, on returning to his work at Lovedale in 1877, placed it under the charge of Dr. Robert Laws, its present head, and the only member of the original pioneering band now remaining in Africa. Under his able administration, and by the indefatigable efforts of him and his colleagues, it has grown up, a bright spot amidst the dark life along the margin of the lake, a centre of Christian civilization, where not only the church and the school, but well-built houses, well-tilled gardens, and a quiet and industrious people, bear witness that the reign of peace and goodwill has begun and the kingdom of God has come.

This, however, has not been achieved without struggle and death—struggle, not with the native tribes, but with the more deadly malaria which haunts the banks of the river and the fever-swept shores of the lake. How terrible that struggle has been is graphically presented by Professor Drummond, when he thus describes a visit he paid to it five years ago:—

"It was a brilliant summer morning when the *Ilala* steamed into Lake Nyasa, and in a few hours we were at anchor in the little bay at Livingstonia. My first impressions of this famous mission-station certainly will never be forgotten. Magnificent mountains of granite, green to the summit with forest, encircled it, and on the silver sand of a still smaller bay stood the small row of trim white cottages. A neat path through a small garden led up to the settlement, and I approached the largest house and entered. It was the Livingstonia Manse—the head missionary's house. It was spotlessly clean; English furniture was in the room, a medicine-chest, familiar-looking dishes were in the cupboards, books lying about, but there was no missionary in it. I went to the next house. It was the school; the benches were there and the blackboard, but there were no scholars and no teacher. I passed to the next. It was the blacksmith's shop; there were the tools and the anvil, but there was no blacksmith. And so on to the next and the next, all in perfect order, and all *empty*. Then a native approached and led me a few yards into the forest; and there, among the mimosa-trees, under a huge granite mountain, were four or five graves. These were the missionaries'. I spent a day or two in the solemn shadow of that deserted manse. It is one of the loveliest spots in the world; and it was hard to believe, sitting under the tamarind-trees by the quiet lake-shore, that the pestilence which walketh at midnight had made this beautiful spot its home."

That was the battle-day. The losses were heavy, men's hearts were tried, but the little band were not dismayed, and this star of Christian promise was not quenched. The station was not deserted, but the missionary centre had by that time been moved from Cape Maclear to Bandawé, 150 miles northward, on the same lake-coast, but somewhat higher up the hill, where the brave missionaries began their task again, the old station being worked by native agents and visited from time to time. Here and at other points along the lake, though often harassed and hindered by native wars and political turmoil, Dr. Laws and his fellow-missionaries have by much patient labour built up a noble Mission, industrial, medical, educational, and evangelistic, and are year by year giving to Africa more and more fully that for which Livingstone hoped and prayed.

Two or three days' journey to the south of Lake

Nyasa lies the mountainous district called by Livingstone the Manganja Highlands, but better known by its more recent name of the Shiré Highlands. These highlands lie to the east of the Cataracts of the Shiré and extend for a considerable distance inland, the ground rising in a succession of terraces. On the third of these terraces, on a breezy upland about 3000 feet above the level of the sea, stands the other Mission which grew out of Captain Young's pioneering expedition. This is *Blantyre*, the African Mission of the Church of Scotland. This is the Mission to the building up of which the three brave missionaries whose story it is the purpose of this little book to tell gave their lives. It may help, therefore, to a clearer appreciation of their work if some slight description of it and its work is given, but this must be reserved to a separate chapter. It may not, however, be out of place here to quote regarding it also the impression formed by Professor Drummond during his visit to Africa. Speaking of it he says:—

"Towards sunset the following evening our caravan filed into Blantyre. On the beauty and interest of this ideal Mission I shall not dwell. But if any one wishes to find out what can be done by broad and practical missionary methods, let him visit the Rev. D. Clement Scott and his friends at Blantyre. . . . I will say of the Livingstonia missionaries and of the Blantyre missionaries, and count it an honour to say it, that they are brave, efficient, single-hearted men, who need our sympathy more than we know, and are equally above our criticism and our praise."

Since these words were written three of those brave, single-hearted men have laid down their lives in the work. Here also the Church has come in answer to the appeal of Livingstone's life, and truly the print of her footsteps has been the graves of her sons.

Close by Blantyre and Livingstonia, and working with them in the interests of Christianity, though not directly part of the Church's missionary organisation, are two Scottish trading companies, *The African Lakes Company* and *Buchanan Brothers*. The former is a trading and carrying company, formed in 1878 with the distinct object of carrying out Livingstone's idea of opening up and developing the regions of East Central Africa from the Zambezi to Tanganyika, making employments for the natives and substituting for the horrible trade by which ivory was formerly brought to the coast a legitimate trade conducted in a Christian spirit, excluding rum and, so far as possible, gunpowder, and strengthening by all its influence the hands of the missionary. This company, whose representatives in Africa are Messrs. John and Fred. Moir, two young Scotchmen, have established stations at various points along the route, and placed steamers both on the Shiré and on Lake Nyasa, their principal station being Mandala (which in the native tongue means "glass"), a place within a mile of Blantyre, and so named by the natives with a reference to the spectacles of Mr. John Moir as the distinguishing feature of the place!

The Messrs. Buchanan are three brothers — also Scotchmen—who have coffee and sugar plantations at Mlungusi, on the slopes of Mount Zomba, about forty miles from Blantyre, and who have been the chief agents in developing the coffee industry in Africa. Besides giving work, with its civilising influences, to a large number of natives, this station forms a centre at which missionary work may be carried on by means of regular Sunday services and a school for the children. Thus are both these companies pouring their influence into the stream of new life that is flowing in for the Christianising of Africa, and are to be numbered among the missionary stars that are already brightening the African night. Two new stars, also, have been lately kindled in the north of Nyasaland, which though as yet faint will by and by brighten the glow of missionary light. Recognising their national responsibility to the peoples of that region now placed under the German Empire, the *Moravian Brethren* and the *Berlin Evangelical Society of the Lutheran Church* have each sent out a little band of eight missionaries—the earnest of more to follow—whose sphere of work is to be in German East Africa, at the north end of Lake Nyasa.

Still more recently another Scottish Presbyterian Mission of a singularly interesting character has been sent out, promoted mainly by members of the British

East African Company, although not directly connected with the Company. On the 6th July 1891, a party of six missionaries—including doctor, teachers and artisans—set out under the leadership of Dr. Stewart of Lovedale, who has done so much for Africa. Already they have reached the Kibwezi River,—a tributary of the Sabaki—a place about 150 miles inland from Mombasa, and here it is proposed to establish a Mission, industrial, educational, evangelistic and medical. An interesting feature which links this with the early days of African Missions is the fact that Dr. Stewart, its leader, was Livingstone's companion in travel; Sir William M'Kinnon, its chairman, is one whose well-known philanthropic efforts on behalf of Africa owe their inspiration to his regard for Livingstone; Mr. A. L. Bruce, its Honorary Secretary and Treasurer, is the son-in-law of Livingstone; and Dr. Robert U. Moffat, its medical officer, is the grandson of Dr. Moffat, the veteran African missionary. As we write, tidings have just arrived of the death of one of the members of its staff—Mr. John Greig, superintendent of its industrial department,—so that here also, as in so many other cases, the land has been claimed by a grave.

Were we to reach forth a little from this heart of Nyasaland we should find ever as we journeyed new stars gleaming through the darkness. North of Lake Nyasa a lofty plateau, cool and healthy, extends for 250 miles to Lake Tanganyika, whose mighty waters stretch for 450 miles farther; and beyond that lies the route to the Victoria Nyanza and the Albert Nyanza. Were we to climb to this plateau we should not only be in touch with all those great lakes, but near us would be the watershed of the mighty Congo. The very mention of these names recalls to our thoughts memories of missionary enterprises glimmering away in the distance like far-off stars in the murky night.

First, like a bright forelight, is the Mission planted on Lake Tanganyika by the *London Missionary Society*—the Society, it will be remembered, which sent Livingstone to Africa at the first. Looking towards it, we recall its story of struggle and trial since the days when, in August 1878, the leader of its first expedition, the Rev. J. B. Thomson, after sixteen weary months of travelling, reached Ujiji, to spend only one short month in the field of his choice ere he was laid in his African grave; to be followed only too soon (the next year) by the Rev. A. W. Dodgshun, who also died at Ujiji seven days after his arrival; and Dr. Mullens, the devoted secretary of the Society, who died while yet only on his way thither. Since that time its chief centre has been removed to Kavala, on the other shore of Lake Tanganyika, where, with the aid of their missionary steamer on the lake, these direct followers of Livingstone are, with life and labour, following up his work.

Beyond that is the field occupied by the *Church Missionary Society*, lying towards the Victoria Nyanza,

C

bright with the names and work of such men as Bishops Hannington and Parker, Dr. John Smith, and Mackay of Uganda, and many another faithful witness and martyr who sealed his testimony with his blood. Facing westward, and looking away far beyond what eye can reach along the line of the Congo, our eyes are towards a region where missionary enthusiasm has multiplied martyrs with a determination and devotion that to some have seemed almost reckless. Thus does a chain of graves stretch over the land, all brightened with the glow of consecrated lives and martyr deaths, and telling at what a cost the Church of Christ has gone forth to the redemption of Africa, answering the appeal which she heard from the lips of the dead Livingstone.

And although we do not attempt to trace the political developments through which it has been brought about, we cannot but remember, and thank God at the remembrance, that after sixteen years' delay—years wherein the missionary and the Christian trader have been preparing the way for it—Nyasaland has become British Central Africa, and now from the Zambezi to Tanganyika the flag of Britain waves over the land in the midst of which the heart of Livingstone is buried, so that in this also the day which he longed to see has dawned.

III.
Blantyre.

III.

BLANTYRE.

BLANTYRE is the first white settlement which the traveller meets in East Central Africa. It is the one star which the Church of Scotland has kindled in the firmament of African Missions in memory of Livingstone, and it was so named after the far-away Lanarkshire village in which he was born. It lies in the heart of the Shiré Highlands, and to reach it the traveller enters Africa from the east coast, sailing up the Zambezi and Shiré. By the recent discovery of the channel through the Chinde mouth, the Zambezi has become an open highway from the ocean, and the tedious delays hitherto occasioned by having to land everything and everybody at Quilimane, sail up the Kwakwa, and then carry overland to the Zambezi will in the near future be avoided. After sailing up the Zambezi for about a hundred miles the traveller comes upon a river which twists away northwards among the mountains. This is the Shiré, one of the tributaries of the Zambezi; but being narrower and deeper in its channel, the tributary is a better stream for navigation than the main river itself. Continuing his journey up the Shiré for a distance of some 160 miles, the traveller reaches a place called Katungas, so named as having been the village of Katunga, a Makololo chief, who had formerly been one of Livingstone's men, and who died only quite recently. This is the landing-place for Blantyre, and here he must disembark, and leaving the river, strike inland, taking on foot a journey of nearly thirty miles steadily uphill all the way, by a hot winding road, passing through pleasing highland scenery, although the chances are that, with his hot tramp under an African sun, he is,—especially during the latter part of his journey,—rather too tired fully to appreciate and enjoy the beauties of the scenery, and it is with a sense of thankfulness and relief that at length he finds himself in Blantyre.

And now, reader, shall I try to describe for you the Blantyre that was or the Blantyre that is?—for indeed they are not the same. It is sixteen years since the foundations of the Mission here were laid. Such a period works great changes on any place. One thinks, for instance, of what changes the last sixteen years have wrought on one's own town or district. But by no such comparison can you form any idea of the changes which these same years have wrought at Blantyre. At home the changes wrought have been on the face and features of things; at Blantyre they have changed the very soul of the place—the habits, the character, the life of the people. I cannot, indeed, show you Blantyre "before it was made," though I

might perhaps try to give you some idea of what they saw who came here sixteen years ago to seek a home for Christianity among these hills. A picturesque country it was into which they came, marked by hills and valleys, with here and there a rocky ravine, through which a mountain burn may be heard gurgling its way to the Shiré, while away in the distance great dark mountains, like the Zomba range and Mount Soche and Ndirandi, each 5000 feet high, may be seen clear on the sky-line.

The country is well wooded, there being wide tracts of forest, though the trees as a rule are not large. The hills are in many instances clothed to the top with dense " bush," denser and darker along the lines of the mountain streams, as you have seen the brushwood marking the course of the burns on the hillsides at home. African villages, many and populous, are to be seen—not bright, tidy, home-like villages such as one sees dotting the landscape from a Scottish hill-top, but clusters of rude mud huts, hiding as it were in the forest, each in terror of the other, and all dreading the slave-raiding Arab, whose visit is ever the precursor of scenes of cruelty and blood.

Life in an African village is a curious kind of existence—a sort of lazy, indifferent, amused contentment. The native has few wants, and is naturally of an indolent, peaceable disposition, having little to compel him to work. He wears next to no clothes, and his food is of the simplest kind. Twice a day he has a big feed of native porridge, made from a kind of millet-seed, to cultivate which only a few weeks' work in the year is required. The women pound it in a big kind of mortar, and do the cooking and other work; while the men, though sometimes doing a little in the way of beating out bark-cloth, weaving cotton, or making baskets, for the most part lounge about talking and smoking. Were you to enter a native village you would probably find a man here and there sitting astride a log of hard wood on the village green, tap, tap, tapping away with his hammer, making his cloth from the Njombo bark, and perhaps a basketmaker at work at the door of his hut; but you would most likely find the chief or headman stretched on the grass under the great council-tree of the village, with most of the men gathered round him, all smoking their *bhang* pipes and talking and joking away, while a huge pot of *pombé*, standing within convenient reach, is appealed to from time to time as the palaver proceeds.

Periodically this easy-going life is rudely broken in upon by a tribal war and the unexpected attack of a hostile tribe, or by the incursion of the Arab slaver, when a fierce excitement takes possession of all and the air of indolent ease gives place to a scene of the wildest confusion.

At the time when the pioneers of the Blantyre Mission appeared there were two distinct tribes of people in the district—the Manganja and the Wayao—

speaking different languages, often at war with one another and among themselves. When Livingstone's Expedition to the Zambezi was recalled in 1863, the Makololo who had accompanied him as porters and carriers settled down on the Shiré, and soon by force of their determined character assumed the chieftainship over the Manganja, who were at the time in danger of being destroyed by the Wayao and the slavers. The Manganja rallied round their new chiefs, and by-and-by the Makololo became a power in the country along the river.

It was to this tribe that Ramukukan, Katunga, Mulilema, and other chiefs, whose names are now familiar in connection with places in the country, belonged, while among the Wayao, chiefs like Kapeni and Malunga were able to hold their own. Besides these two tribes, however, another people, wild and war-like, dwelt in the hill-country away to the northwest beyond the Shiré. These were the Angoni, and from time to time they came down in fierce raids and swept across both the Yao and the Manganja, who lived in terror of them and fled from their villages at the rumour of their approach. Many a bloody war and blackened stretch of country testified to the fierce character of these Angoni chiefs and their warriors when on the war-path.

This, then, was the country and such were the people to whom the Scottish missionaries came in 1875. This is Blantyre as it was before it was Blantyre! I shall not attempt to describe for you in detail the work which the missionaries did in those early days—how, when sick and weary with their journey up the river, they began to clear and level a site for a mission-station, and to erect dwellings for themselves, houses of bamboos and grass and mud, which they were to try in future to call by the name of home!— how they overcame the prejudices and secured the confidence of the natives, and induced them by the offer of yards of calico as payment to come and join them in learning to work and to continue at work. This they did with such success that it was not long till every Monday morning saw a crowd of both men and women waiting eager to be hired for work in laying out the station, making roads, building houses preparing the garden, hoeing the fields. A series of terraces was made. Water was brought a distance of two miles, and irrigation made easy—an invaluable element in the development of Blantyre. In conjunction with the Livingstonia Mission, a road was surveyed and made from the station southwards to Ramukukan's, at the foot of the cataracts on the river, a distance of some thirty miles, and another of greater length northward to the Upper Shiré.

I cannot wait to speak as I should like of the first experiments in gardening and agriculture, the sowing of various seeds, and the patient waiting to see whether anything would grow, and if so, what. Very interesting, too, is the story of four little slips which Mr.

Duncan, the gardener, took out with him from the Botanic Gardens in Edinburgh—one tea and three coffee plants. If these would grow, how much it might mean for the new country! Carefully they were tended, and anxiously watched and watered; and we can understand with what feelings those who watched them saw first one, then another, then another of them die. Only one little tiny struggling slip was left, and it looked as if it were to die too; but it didn't—it lived; and that one little slip has grown into the coffee plantations, not only of the Mission at Blantyre, but of Buchanan Brothers at Zomba, of the African Lakes Company at Mandala, and of Messrs. Sharrer, Duncan, and others, till in this year (1891) we learn that the Messrs. Buchanan have in their plantations alone 1,000,000 coffee-plants, and that the highest price quoted in the London market for the season has been for this very Shiré Highland coffee! That little tiny slip, so feeble-looking, and once so nearly dead, yet so marvellously fruitful, is a fit emblem of the Mission itself.

I cannot wait, either, to speak of the *personnel* of the Mission—of the brave men and women by whose life and labour it has been built up. Henry Henderson, as has been said, was its pioneer and guide. In its earliest days the Free Church missionaries at Livingstonia lent it valuable aid, Dr. Stewart visiting it in 1877, and during a stay of three months helping to organise the work; while his relative, Mr. James Stewart, C.E., who accompanied him, directed the laying out of the place and the making of the road. The Rev. Duff Macdonald, B.D., its first ordained missionary, went out in 1878, Mrs. Macdonald being the first white woman the natives had ever seen. Dr. T. T. Macklin was its first medical missionary. Mr. Buchanan, now of Zomba, and Mr. Jonathan Duncan, the gardeners, began the work of cultivation in garden and field.

Around these and their companions the natives gathered, settling in villages on the Mission ground. At the close of each day all the workers, summoned by a bugle-call, gathered together to listen to a Gospel address—"a talk about God." A school was begun for the boys, conducted in a little grass-roofed building, where also every Sunday the little community gathered together for Christian worship.

So the work grew and extended, additional missionaries coming out from time to time to strengthen the staff. The Mission, however, was not without its dark days, times of trouble and anxiety, when it seemed as if it might even be necessary to retire altogether from the field so hopefully occupied. In 1879-80 it was shaken to its very foundations by troubles arising out of a policy which acted on Livingstone's idea of regarding the Mission as a *Colony* as well as a Church, and the exercise of a jurisdiction based upon that idea. Very sad and trying were the experiences of that time, but there is no need to recount them here. The storm passed, the night wore away, and the work was not destroyed. On the contrary, the Church at home addressed herself anew to it in a spirit of chastened earnestness, and it seemed as if the sun of a new morning shone out when in the summer of 1881 the Rev. David Clement Scott, B.D., and his brave young wife, accompanied by a medical missionary, went forth to gather together the shaken elements of the Mission, and proceed with the task of founding and building up in the territory of a native chief a Christian Church, not a British colony. How nobly they have discharged the trust committed to them no words of mine can fully tell.

In 1884 the sky darkened again over the Mission. Three times in succession during that year not only the interests of the Mission but also the lives of the missionaries were seriously endangered, first, by disturbances consequent on the murder of Chipetula, a Makololo chief, then through a revolt of the Machinjiri against the Portuguese, and lastly by a fierce raid of the warlike Angoni on the Yaos and Chipetas in the neighbourhood of Blantyre. During this last, the calm courage of Mr. Scott and his wife, who, accompanied by Dr. Peden, undertook a journey of three hundred miles to brave the fierce Angoni chief in his own land and in the midst of his armed warriors, so impressed the chief that the attack was averted and the raid of 4000 Angoni warriors sweeping across the Shiré Highlands was turned aside from the villages around Blantyre. Since then the endurance, the resources, and the tact of the missionaries have been tried again and again by the political complications, the Arab wars, and the Portuguese difficulties which have so largely made up the history of these recent years. Often they have been for months cut off from all communication with the coast and with home. At times the difficulties of the situation have been very great and the strain of suspense and anxiety very heavy. Sorrow, too, and death have crossed their path, but they have never lost heart; their faith in God has never failed, their love for Africa has never grown cold, and the work of the Mission has never stood still. Through storm and sunshine its growth has steadily continued. Already new stations are beginning to grow up around it. At Domasi, away beyond Mount Zomba, near Lake Shirwa, fifty-five miles from the parent Mission, a new station was started some years ago under the charge of the Rev. Alexander Hetherwick, M.A., F.R.G.S. It is situated in the midst of the Yao tribe, and in both its methods and spirit is a true child of Blantyre. It has church and school, as well as hoeing, planting, building, &c., with which to train and help the natives. At Chirazulo, too, as will be found in the story of Robert Cleland, a new post has been occupied and a new centre of Christian life planted; while at Mount Milanji, also, the field has been surveyed and the land claimed by the sacrifice of a life. I wish, reader, I could close this chapter by taking you to have one look at Blantyre as it is to-day, through the patient endurance and the much Christian labour of these sixteen years.

Blantyre stands to-day where it did on the lofty plateau, but you would hardly recognise the old place. There now passes through it the well-made road from Katungas, on the river below the cataracts, to Matope on the Upper Shiré—the route along which all who are bound for the great Central Lakes must pass. It thus occupies an important position on the direct highway into Central Africa, and every traveller going thither passes through it. Approaching it now, we pass along an avenue, nearly a mile in length, of tall beautiful Eucalyptus trees (blue gums) planted in 1879, and already many of them sixty feet high, with a clean, well-kept road between them. Passing through these we find ourselves in a large open square, in the centre of which stands a handsome church, just completed, and which by its beauty at once arrests the attention of the traveller and strikes him with astonishment. We pass on in the meantime, however, for we must return and take a leisurely view of it. On one side of the square, on a terraced slope, lies a garden planted with fruit-trees and vegetables, and bright with flowers both European and indigenous. Grouped around the square on its other sides are the school, the Manse,—with its thatched roof and wide verandahs,—the houses of the doctor and the other missionaries, the joiner's workshop, the smithy, the zinc-roofed store, &c. The square itself is tidy and trim-looking, ornamental trees here and there, while the Manse garden is bright with geraniums, roses, dahlias, and other English flowers, as well as tall shrubs and gay flowering creepers. As we pass along, we hear the ring of the hammer on the anvil and the sound of the carpenter's saw and plane, and we learn that it is the brown Manganja hand that is wielding these. We see numbers of native men and women, clean and tidy-looking in their white calicoes, busy at work in the garden, or "hoeing" in the fields belonging to the Mission farm behind the houses. As we pass through the square we may take a look into the school. Here we find over two hundred boys and girls, some of them day-scholars, and others boarders who have been sent by their parents from villages at a distance, many of them being sons of chiefs. When one thinks that by-and-by these will be chiefs themselves, one feels how important is the work of the Christian schoolmaster here. It reminds one of Luther's schoolmaster lifting his hat to his boys for what they might one day be. We find the classes going on just as we see them do in a school at home. The children are smart and learn easily. They are taught not only to read and write, both in their own language and in English, but also grammar, history, arithmetic, &c., and we can see for ourselves, as we look at their copybooks, writing and figures that few children in our Scottish schools could beat. There are altogether, besides the European missionaries, some twenty native teachers; and as one looks at their brown faces and dark, black eyes one's thoughts go back to the time, only sixteen years ago, when these young men and women were playing around the mud-huts of an African village, before Blantyre was there. What a change!

Suddenly a bugle-note rings out. It is half-past one; and immediately we see, from garden and field and workshop and school, men, women, and children gather together. It is the hour for the daily midday service, which all the workers on the station attend. It is a simple native service, a hymn, a short address, and prayer, taken by the members of the Mission and by the native teachers in turn. The hours of work are 6 to 11 A.M. and 2 to 5 P.M., and all who come to work assemble daily for this service before going out to the work of the afternoon. In this way the gospel is preached to every one who comes to work in the service of the Mission, and some of these workers come from places from five to a hundred miles distant, some coming even from Angoniland. The other regular services in the Mission are, daily native service in the morning, and an English service every evening, besides the four services on Sunday.

We cannot wait now to follow these workers as they disperse to their different departments of work, though each of these would furnish much that would interest. Nor can we go to the Manse to see the class for sewing, &c., which at this hour Mrs. Scott will be conducting in the verandah; nor to the laundry to see

D

how beautifully these African women and girls have learned to do such work as is done there.

But we must not turn away without pausing to let our thoughts rest, if only for an instant, on the handsome church, so striking in appearance, and which means so much. Standing there in the midst of the square, it is not only, in its elegance and beauty, the most striking feature in Blantyre, but it is a signal token of the progress of the Mission. I shall not attempt to describe it, with its pillars and arches and towers and dome, so harmonious in proportions and so ornate in design. The accompanying illustration will perhaps serve better to give some idea of it. The *Illustrated London News*, in which a picture of it appeared in August last, spoke of it as "an edifice which would be creditable to any town or city in Great Britain, and which is said, truly for aught we know, to be the handsomest church in Africa, including such cities as Cape Town, Port Elizabeth, and Durban." But to me it seems that far better than the beauty of the building is the testimony it bears to the marvellous work which, by the grace of God, the missionaries at Blantyre have been able to do in Central Africa. We have just been telling how, when they came to these Shiré Hills, they found Yao and Manganja at war with one another, while the fierce Angoni were the terror of both. Now here is a church constructed entirely by native labour. Mr. Scott was his own architect, and with the assistance of Mr.

MANGANJA AND YAO.

M'Ilwain, artisan missionary, and his neighbour, Mr. Buchanan of Zomba, the master-builder as well; but the native Africans did the work, making their own bricks, burning their own lime, hewing their own timber, and, in short, building their own church, the building materials, which are of the best quality, being obtained wholly from the district, except the glass and some internal fittings. Nor is this all. It occupied three years in building, and during that time Yao and Manganja and Angoni have been living and working and worshipping together. Together, in more senses than one, they have been building the Church of God. In the words of *The Mission Record*, "The brickmakers and bricklayers, the pointers and the carpenters, were Yao and Manganja men trained in the Mission. The hewers of wood and drawers of water were the Angoni. They laid aside their spears and shields for the hoe and the pick. Instead of plundering the native granaries, they carried the bricks and the mortar; instead of spreading the desolation of war and carrying off the captives to slavery, they helped to build the temple of the God of peace, where the slave may hear the glorious gospel of freedom in Christ Jesus." Truly it is the doing of the Lord and wondrous in our eyes.

What a delight it would be if one could go to spend a Sunday in Blantyre! How it would bring one into touch with the work of God if one could see the native congregation assemble for morning service in that beautiful church at 8.30, then join in the worship of the English congregation at eleven, visit the Sunday-school in the Manse at three, or accompany the evangelists, who at that hour go out into the villages round about preaching the Gospel of the Kingdom, and then close the day in the quiet worship of the evening service at half-past six. What a busy, worshipful, Christ-like life is theirs!

But what must it have been to be present at the service of Holy Communion on the first Sunday in the new church, to feel the touch of the impressive stillness and taste the joy of its worship, and join the company that sat down together at the Holy Table— not only the missionary and the traveller and the explorer and the trader, but—most blessed of all— thirty of these native Africans, humble Christian communicants in the Church of God, sitting down together with those who came bringing them the glad tidings in the fellowship of the one faith and the one Lord and Redeemer! Ay! and more also. It was for this that Henry Henderson, John Bowie, and Robert Cleland had laboured and died. Blessed dead! They rest from their labours and their works do follow them. Surely they too, in their glorified rest, had a share in the joy of that day of reaping, when the fruits of their toil were seen. Blessed be God for the communion of saints in heaven and on earth!

IV.
Henry Henderson,
THE PIONEER.

MR. AND MRS. HENDERSON.

IV.

HENRY HENDERSON.

HENRY HENDERSON was a son of the Manse, his father being the late Rev. Dr. Henderson of Kinclaven, in Perthshire, where he was born in 1843. The old church and Manse stand in a charming rural spot close by the Tay, without even a village near, so that his earliest impressions of God's great world were gathered from a beautiful picture of field and wood and river, with the blue hills behind,—the stillness unbroken by the roar of the city, and God's clear sky undimmed by any cloud of earthly smoke. It was no wonder that all his life he loved to be where Nature's book was open to him, and that he could never feel at home among the restraints of city life.

He received the godly and hardy upbringing which so often has made the sons of the Manse the men they are. His father, who was somewhat of the sterner type of the old school, taught his sons himself till they were fourteen, and then sent them off to school and college; but to Henry, who was the youngest, there was perhaps less of stern severity shown than to the others. Being without companions of his own age, he was much with his father, to whom he became useful in many respects. As a boy he was thoughtful and sagacious, and rather quaint in his ways, often causing amusement to the other members of the family. All his life he was most conscientious and rigidly honest, never pretending to be better than he really was. He was not over-fond of prolonged study, and was always ready to take part in outdoor occupations, caring little what remarks might be made about him provided what he was doing were necessary or useful. Much amusement was caused one winter, when, the office of beadle having become vacant—rather a despised office in those days—Harry, then a boy of thirteen, offered to ring the church bell and carry up the Bible to the pulpit, only stipulating that he should carry up the Bible before the people came into church. His offer was accepted, and for a whole winter he discharged the duty quite readily. About the same time one of the parish "bodies" said to him she supposed he would be going to be a minister, but his reply was prompt and characteristic. "No," he said, "I am not. I can't take care of my own soul, and how could I take care of the souls of other people?" The same tone of mind and feeling continued when the time came for him to decide on his future career. He could not be induced to enter the ministry, doubting his own motives and dreading a responsibility so great. At the age of sixteen he went to the University of Edinburgh, where he passed through a full Arts course in a manner which gave promise of useful work in any profession which he might have adopted. But he did not feel that any of the professions offered the sphere of service for which he was fitted. His inborn love of travel and adventure led him to look abroad, and accordingly at the age of twenty, furnished with a few letters of introduction, he set forth to seek his fortune in Queensland. He was fortunate in getting good situations, and for twelve years he remained in the bush, seeing a great deal of bush-life. If he had chosen he might have established his fortunes there, for his character and powers were such that he was soon trusted, and offers were made to him which most men would have accepted, and which, in the prosperous days twenty years ago, would certainly have led him to wealth. At one time there joined him two young men from home, both gentlemen's sons, and perhaps it was in observing them that he was able clearly to study himself. Anyhow, he soon came to feel that all of them were out of their proper sphere. It was not long till one of them returned home, and after a course of study became a clergyman of the Church of England. The other also came home, and soon after died; while Henderson, having grown year by year more dissatisfied with the selfishness and self-seeking of a colonist's life of that time, felt within him a growing desire for a life in which he would have greater opportunities of usefulness and of benefiting his fellow-creatures—for some form of service, if possible, in which he might help the spread of Christianity. In the hope of finding some such sphere he returned home. He again enrolled himself as a student in one or two of the classes in Edinburgh University, thinking it might possibly prove useful to him in some way. Here again, like an attractive vision, the idea of the ministry presented itself to him, but again harassed with doubts as to his fitness for it, he abandoned the idea. More than a year he had passed thus, hoping and waiting for some path of usefulness to open up to him, when one day in the Advocates' Library he happened to turn over the pages of the *Missionary Record*, and read of a proposal to organise a Mission to Central Africa as the Church of Scotland's memorial to Dr. Livingstone, and of the desire to find some one who would go as a pioneer to prepare the way for it. Like a flash of inspiration, or a voice from God, came the thought that here was the opportunity he had been waiting for. He could not be a minister, but he could be a pioneer missionary. He had learned what it was to "rough it" in the Australian bush. He could wander over lonely hills; he could sleep under the stars; he could endure hunger and fatigue, and could turn his hand to anything that needed to be done. Here was a chance of serving his Church, serving his fellow-men, serving Christ. He would go to Africa to open the way for others, and as a missionary live a Christian life among the heathen. God's pillar of cloud before him was moving forward, and he would follow it; so he offered himself to the Committee of this African Mission, of which the late Dr. Macrae, Hawick, was convener, and his services were gladly accepted. The Foreign Mission Committee of the Free Church, largely inspired by the enthusiasm of the Rev. James Stewart (now Dr. Stewart of Lovedale), was organising an advance party to visit the shores of Lake Nyasa and select a site where a Mission party, to go out the following year, might take up their headquarters. No sooner had this been determined on than the Reformed Presbyterian Church, the Church of Scotland, and the United Presbyterian Church all requested to be allowed to have a share in the movement; and surely it was a token for good that the Scottish Churches could thus unite for such a work. The United Presbyterian Church, though precluded by other responsibilities from undertaking missionary work in Central Africa, generously placed at the disposal of the Free Church Committee, for a time at least, the services of the Rev. Dr. Robert Laws, a medical missionary, who had been intended for service in another field; and the Church of Scotland, already preparing to plant a Mission in the neighbourhood of Lake Nyasa, requested that their pioneer missionary might be allowed to accompany the expedition and receive from it such assistance as it might be in the power of its members to render. That pioneer was Henry Henderson. Few men could have been found better fitted for such a work. It was just the kind of work in which he had spent the last twelve years in the Australian bush. And yet he often spoke of it as a strange reversal of the kind of life he had at first planned out for himself. He had always shrunk from the idea of having to deal with uncivilised races. It was for that reason he had gone to Queensland, where there was least chance of contact with aboriginal tribes. Now he found himself despatched to a land where he would be plunged alone, perhaps for years, into the heart of the life which he felt would try him more than any other. How often do we find that that from which a man naturally shrinks turns out to be the calling whereunto God has called him!

The expedition, which was placed under the command of Mr. E. D. Young, R.N., included, besides Dr. Laws and Mr. Henderson, a carpenter, two engineers, an agriculturist, and a seaman of the royal navy, eight good men and true, who bravely discharged the commission entrusted to them. They sailed from London on the 20th May 1875, and on the 23rd July they cast anchor in the Kongone mouth of the Zambezi. The first duty enjoined on them was to launch on Lake Nyasa a steamer which they had brought out with them, built for the purpose, and named the *Ilala* after the place where Livingstone had died. They landed her on the beach at the Kongone mouth, steered her through the shallows of the Zambezi and the Shiré, unscrewed her into eight hundred pieces at the Murchison Falls, and had these pieces carried on the heads of an army of eight hundred natives over a roadless track for upwards of sixty miles, not one single piece being wanting at the journey's end. There they reconstructed the steamer and launched her again on the Upper Shiré. It was a lovely morning, the 12th of October, when with a gentle breeze the *Ilala* rode over the swell as the great blue waters of Nyasa received the first steam-vessel that had ever entered an African lake. "God speed you," said Mr. Young reverently. "Amen," responded his companions. Then they sang a hymn together, and a service of devout thanksgiving was conducted on the deck of the little vessel. The African stillness was broken by a new song, even praise to our God, and the dream of Livingstone for the healing of Africa began to be a reality. Of the brave men who stood there that day only one—Dr. Laws of Bandawe—now remains in Africa, left alone since they laid Henry Henderson to his rest in the cemetery at Quilimane.

In all the work of this memorable expedition Henderson had his full share. Six days later he was present when the foundations of Livingstonia, the station of the Free Church Mission, were laid at Cape Maclear; and when the work of station-building was fairly begun, he started, along with Dr. Laws and Mr. Young, on a voyage of exploration round the lake, his Committee's instructions to him being to proceed first to Lake Nyasa. The hardships and privations of that voyage are well told by Mr. Young in his "Journal of a Mission to Nyasa." The tremendous gales and fearful seas which they encountered justified the title which Livingstone had given to it, "the Lake of Storms." Then the vessel was small and the accommodation limited. There was a narrow space between the gunwale of the vessel and the cabin-wall, and into this Henderson had to squeeze himself every night; and ever afterwards, until improvements altered the plan of the vessel, this hole was called "Henderson's Coffin." Hunger, too, was added to other discomforts, and provisions were dealt out with a sparing hand. On one occasion Henderson was driven by hunger to barter his handkerchief at a village where they stopped for a mess of native porridge and rotten fish. But all privations were taken without complaint as part of the contract. His examination of the shores of the lake satisfied him that it was unsuitable for European occupation, so he resolved to turn back and explore the Shiré Highlands, the mountainous district to the south-east of the lake. These Livingstone had always praised, and thither the great traveller had himself led the first Central African Mission of the English Universities. That Mission had had to be abandoned, leaving the graves of the noble Bishop M'Kenzie and his three companions; but kindly memories of "the English" still lived among the native inhabitants. To that district Henderson accordingly turned. The *Ilala* brought him down as far as Nsapa, on the Upper Shiré, and from there, with Tom Bokwito (a freed slave of the old Bishop M'Kenzie days) as his interpreter, and four native carriers to carry his loads, he started to explore the Shiré Hills. And now he was indeed on that strange and lonely path which God had marked for him to be his own. Round the north side of Mount Zomba he went. He stayed for some days with an old chief, Malemya, close to where Domasi Station now stands; then he journeyed on to the neighbourhood of Mount Chirazulo. Everywhere the natives flocked to gaze upon the first white man they had ever seen. At Ngludi Hill (near Soche) the illness of his servant kept him for ten days, and gave him a good opportunity of familiarising himself with the district. The headman of the village sent him on to his chief, Kapeni, then living on the slopes of Mount Ndirande. Everything seemed favourable, and everywhere he was welcomed. Gradually but surely the feeling deepened on his spirit that he was now in the neighbourhood of the place he was in search of. He was on the high, healthy plateau, and yet within easy reach of the river, the means of communication with the coast. The natives were eager that the English should come to stay among them, for they would protect them from the marauding Angoni, before whose raids they had been driven to these hills. The natives guided him to several likely spots, and from these he selected two, either of which would be suitable. With his mind so far made up, but leaving the final decision till he should return with the members of the Mission party, whose arrival was now almost due, he made his way down towards the river. About three miles from his camp on Mount Ndirando he halted to lunch under the shade of a large tree on the banks of a stream. On the ridge above him were the ruins of a native village whose inhabitants had fled from fear of the Angoni. One solitary hut remained, inhabited by an old woman, whom neither the fear of wild beasts nor fear of the still wilder Angoni had been able to drive from what she called her home. Henderson sat there under that great tree, looking at this ridge and the ruined huts that crowned it. It was one of the two sites he had fixed on. Blantyre Church, schoolhouses, garden, work-shops, and coffee-fields crown it to-day. The wilderness and the solitary place are glad, and the desert rejoices and blossoms as the rose.

Thus it was that Henderson chose the site of Blantyre. Not long ago, before the sad tidings of his death had come, the author of "Light in Africa"—himself one who had spent twelve years in an African mission-field—said to me, "I do not know whether your Church recognises her indebtedness to Henry Henderson or not, but even if he had done nothing but chosen the site of Blantyre, that itself would have been worthy to be a life's work." The site, in the opinion of all who have visited it, is singularly well chosen. The ground rises from the river in a succession of terraces, and Blantyre is on the third of these, about 3000 feet above the sea. Gushing springs and flowing streams abound, the scenery is beautiful and picturesque, the soil is fertile, there is abundance of good timber, the chiefs are friendly, the people are willing to receive instruction, and the climate is unusually healthy. In the words of Livingstone, "it needs no quinine." Even in presence of the recent melancholy events, we must not forget that the Mission had been fifteen years there without one single death that could be attributed to the climate.

Having determined on the site, Henderson took up his quarters in Ramukukan's village, among the Makololo, on the Lower Shiré, to await the coming of the expected Mission party. And wearily he had to wait, day after day and week after week. The fever that haunts the river caught him, and for days he was confined to his hut, all alone in his weakness, his only companions his New Testament, the "Christian Year," and a volume of Cowper's Poems. Each day his plate of native porridge and beans was cooked and brought to him by one of the chief's wives. Thus week after week passed without tidings of the expected party, till three months had gone. Then he borrowed a canoe from the chief and set off down the river in search of news of them. All the way to the Kongone mouth he went, only to spend another weary month of idle waiting there. He was ill; a single tin of sardines was all the English food he had with him. Native food was scarce and dear, and his troubles threatened to become worse, when news came that the party had

E

arrived at Quilimane, and were on their way up the Kwakwa to join him on the Zambezi. Great was their disappointment when they learned that not Lake Nyasa but the Shiré Hills was to be the site of the future Mission. The succeeding days were days of trial and worry and disappointment and fever. They ascended the river in boats and canoes, the only means of communication in those days, but it was slow and weary work. Ultimately they reached Ramukukan's, and here Henderson left the others while he ascended the hills to make preparation for their coming in a day or two. Several of the half-ruined huts were repaired, and on the 23rd October 1876 the remainder of the Mission party came up, took possession and founded Blantyre. Once they were well settled Henderson considered his task done and returned home for a time, He had found what he had been sent to seek—a site for a Mission. Two years later, however, saw him again in Africa, and, with intervals of two visits home and a short visit to a brother in India, he remained there till his death. His heart was in the Mission and his hand was ready to serve it. It would be difficult to say what was his department or what it was exactly that he did. He always shrank from the responsibility of fixed and definite work. He was no public speaker and did not preach, but he had a grand ideal of what the Mission life should be—a stooping-down to live a Christ-like life among the native people. He supplied that which is of such importance in any

Mission, and especially in a Mission like Blantyre. He was always everywhere, seeing that everything and everybody was right. The natives called him by a name which meant "the man who never sleeps." If goods had to be brought up from the river, he would see about it; if something were wanted for the school, or the church, or the work-shops, or the garden, or the cattle, Mr. Henderson was the man to look to for it. If a chief had to be treated with, or a village trouble arranged, or a gap anywhere to be filled, or an *ulendo* (a journey) undertaken, or any special work to be done at home in Blantyre, in the bush, or on the march, Mr. Henderson was always ready. It is impossible to overestimate what he was to the Mission—a wise and judicious counsellor and an unfailing help in any time of need.

The last time I saw him was in February 1888, the day on which, in the little Scotch church in Caledonian Road, London, I married him to Miss Harriet Bowie, the younger sister of Mrs. D. Clement Scott. Oh, how proud he looked that day standing by the bright, brave young wife who was going to share with him the cares of the Mission in that African home! As on a new lease of service he went forth again, the spirit of such willing service being abundantly shared by his gifted wife. Wherever they were needed,—in whatever part of the work they could be of most service,—that was where they both desired to be. This was the law of life for them both. And what a vast field of usefulness does such a readiness open up in a place like Blantyre, where there are so many little things to be seen to that do not technically belong to anybody in particular, but are for the help and comfort of all!

"We have as yet made Blantyre our headquarters," he wrote after returning, "contenting ourselves with two trips—one to Chirazulo and one to Milanje. It is our intention to go to Domasi soon, at least for a week or two, to see if we can be of use there in any way. I believe the place would be much benefited by a white woman being there, if only for the sake of the bachelors, who are not always able to look to their own comforts." They went to Domasi, and the weeks lengthened out into months, and the presence of the white woman, so bright and capable, so thoughtful for every one, and so industrious and practical, came like a fountain of refreshing to the little community there. They made a trip to Milanje, where the presence of Mrs. Henderson was taken as a guarantee that their errand was a peaceful one, and they were well received both by the chief and his people.

After some time they returned to Blantyre, where they were both greatly wanted for the ever-increasing demands of the work there. Most heartily they threw themselves into it, and many a graphic picture of life in that hive of industry came home, flashed in quick touches in the personal letters of the clever young wife. "Every one here is as busy as can be," she wrote. "There is endless work, and the *sweating system* is in vogue! Most of the wives in Blantyre will be able soon to take medals as either charwomen, bakers, laundresses, &c., and two of them would be able to qualify at once as skeletons! You can have no idea of the work. It is delightful work, and we all enjoy it, but all the same it is very hard. . . . We have started 'the Blantyre Laundry,' with one customer to begin with. Mr. Buchanan is making a large table, and we hope to get lots of irons, &c., from home. We will not, however, enlarge our custom till Mrs. Fenwick returns. Wonders are going to happen then. Just now is the trying season of the year. Every one is more or less 'seedy' except myself. Mrs. Scott is too hard-worked, and Mrs. Tanner has been ill for weeks. The doctor fears she may have to go home unless she picks up, as we all hope she will in the cold season. Yet, with it all, life out here is just delightful. How thoroughly you would enjoy it and enter into it!" Occasionally clouds of anxiety hovered over them, and such touches came in as, "This mail has brought us sad news from Uganda. We are well off here, at least in the meantime;" or again, "The news from the river is rather disquieting again. These troubles with the Portuguese keep us all anxious."

By-and-by the birth of a son brought a new joy into the home of the pioneer missionary and his wife, and very proud and happy they were in this gift of God. "The Boy Henderson," as they playfully called him, or "the Little Cardinal" (so Mr. Hetherwick entitled him), with his rosy, chubby cheeks and bright eyes, was a new centre of attraction in the little community, and the growth of motherhood in the young mother's heart seemed to deepen her affection for the little black children that were her special care.

From one of her latest letters we may quote the following glimpse of a woman's work in the missionary home:—"We have a great many girls just now," she writes, "somewhere about sixty—fourteen of them from the river. Four of them arrived yesterday who had been away since the death of Katunga (a Makololo chief who had been one of Livingstone's men). We did not expect them back. Then, when Masea sent his five daughters back after the holidays, he sent five daughters of his different headmen along with them. We have great difficulty in disposing of them at night. In fact, we have, as it were, to pack them in at night and unpack them in the morning! The dormitory is far too small. These girls all live in the house, and about twenty-five boys as well, so you may understand how Mr. Waddell (a visitor) thought this an interesting place. He came into contact with the children a great deal, for they run about the house. About a dozen of these girls are finished with school and do industrial work, most of them in the laundry, as well as house-work. The children are what one might call 'jolly,'—full of fun and brightness—that is, the majority of them. Never a meal passes, almost, at which we have not some bit of fun to tell about them.

"Dressing all these children is quite a thought—where to get clothes for them all. The mission-boxes are very nice, but the clothes last no time; the sun rots them, and we are continually making new garments. Just now we have set ourselves—Mrs. Fenwick, Bella (Mrs. Scott), and I—to make one shirt each for so many days till we get all the boys clothed. I have the boys in charge for dressing and washing. The latter is a lengthy process just at present. They have to be washed in hot water and carbolic and rubbed with sulphur ointment—treatment for an irruption they have, I tell them, with eating too much(!), at which they laugh derisively. I don't think there could be a nicer place to work in than here."

Thus time went on, and for nearly three years they laboured lovingly together, and then with almost tropical suddenness the shadows fell, and without a twilight the night came. Henderson caught fever when on a journey down at the river. The attack was pretty severe, and the malaria hung about him, but neither he nor his wife thought it more serious than the usual fever caught on the river. His wife could write:—"I am sorry to say Harry is not at all well. He looks as yellow as a lemon. Jack (Dr. Bowie) has given him a tonic and a bottle of port. He ought to take a glass and a half a day, but it is amusing to hear his dodges to avoid taking it: 'I think I will take a little milk instead,' or 'a lemon drink,' and so on. Jack thinks he ought to leave before the hot weather comes; he himself is anxious to try another year. I tell him people will think he is baby's great-grandfather. He looks about 150 years old just now! He is so thin, too, and yellow and shrivelled up, and altogether miserable. He is so different these last few months from what he used to be. The least thing tires him, even going to Mandala; and before, he used never to be in, but was always walking about the place. Probably he will be himself soon again." Ah! never again, bright young wife! There is that coming which will be harder on him than the fever-fiend of the river, but you will not be there to see him reel and fall from the blow.

By-and-by the doctor ordered him home, assuring him that if another attack came he could not weather it. With great reluctance and disappointment of heart they began preparations for returning home for good. Then came the terrible diphtheria, of which the next chapter tells. It took from him within ten days first his child, and then his wife, and then his brother-in-law, Dr. Bowie, and left him shattered in health and broken in spirit, to start for this country. Before he left, he slipped away alone to pay a last sad visit to the little cemetery where his beloved had been laid. It was no wonder that as he knelt by the fresh graves the storm of grief swayed through him like an autumn wind through the leafless trees. He was able, however, to take charge of the home-coming party during the journey down the river with his usual care, and he seemed the better for the occupation which it gave him.

At Quilimane there was a short delay waiting for a steamer, and while there the dreaded fever came again. He was in the house of Mr. Ross, agent of the African Lakes Company, where he had every possible kindness; and both Dr. Henry of the Livingstonia Mission, who was his fellow-traveller, and the doctor at Quilimane, did him everything that human skill and care could do, but in vain. God's time was come. The day's toil was over, his wanderings were at an end, and very gently, very softly, like a little child, he literally fell asleep. Not a word of farewell, not a struggle, not even a sigh, but in the sweet peace of God the eyes closed and the weary traveller was at rest, the sorrowful spirit was comforted, the divided family was reunited, and were together in the heavenly home. Well done, good and faithful servant; enter thou into the joy of thy Lord!

They buried him in the cemetery at Quilimane, and thus he lies at the gateway of Nyasaland, Europe and Africa alike mourning his loss. Among many tokens of the regard in which he was held, at home as well as abroad, none was more touching than the graceful tribute which two of the Judges of the Court of Session in Edinburgh paid to the memory of their old college friend. In the Parish Church of Kinclaven, by the winding Tay, there may now be seen a Memorial Tablet bearing the following inscription:—

HENRY HENDERSON,
Pioneer of the Church of Scotland's Mission at Blantyre, in East Africa.
Son of the late Rev. H. Henderson, D.D., Minister of this Parish.
Born at the Manse, April 14, 1843.
Died at Quilimane, February 12, 1891.
And there buried.

This tablet was erected by his old college friends, the Right Honourable J. P. B. Robertson, M.P., Lord Advocate of Scotland, and Lord Stormonth Darling, to commemorate in the church of his native parish a life of enterprise, gentleness, courage, self-denial, and absolute devotion to the service of Almighty God.

"*If any man serve Me, him will My Father honour.*"
—St. John xii. 26.

V.

Dr. John Bowie,
MEDICAL MISSIONARY.

IV.

DR. JOHN BOWIE.

THE son of a much-respected citizen of Edinburgh (Mr. Henry Bowie, long secretary of the Philosophical Institution), Dr. Bowie was as truly a representative of the city as Henry Henderson was of the country, for all his life till he went to Africa he had been accustomed to a city life. Born in 1858, he was an only son, but had three sisters, two of whom (Mrs. D. C. Scott and Mrs. Henderson), along with himself, have given their lives to Africa. His first step on the ladder was taken when, as a little boy of five, he went with his two sisters to a lady's school at Wardie, taught by a Miss Baird, a relative of General Baird of Indian celebrity. Who that saw the quiet, shy little fellow in those days would have dreamed that a time would come when that boy would step aside from a place in the foremost rank of his profession that he might, Christ-like, spend and be spent for the redemption of Africa; and that one day men would hold their breath as they read how, away in that far-off land, he died for others, with the courage of a hero, the spirit of a martyr, and the devotion of a saint?

When he outgrew this school he passed through the High School of Edinburgh, and subsequently went to business, obtaining an appointment in an office in Leith. It is said of him as a boy that among strangers he was quiet and retiring, and no one who saw him thus would have fancied that he had any fun in him at all. But see him at home romping with his sisters and he was very different. There he was full of fun,—an inveterate tease to them, keeping them always lively, and it was no wonder that they were devoted to him and all their lives were proud of *Jack*. On leaving school they had sent him to business, but his heart was elsewhere, and he had other dreams of life. One day he came home, and, to his father's surprise, announced that he had passed the medical preliminary examination, and begged that he might be allowed to become a medical student. His father, seeing how his heart was set on it, wisely acceded to his request, and he went to college, where he worked very hard and with great success.

In the glimpses we get of him at this time we can trace a blending of qualities that afterwards made him what he was in Africa. He was at once the simple, light-hearted, child-like boy and the earnest and enthusiastic student. A friend and playmate of those days writes:—"He worked very hard, and was most interested and enthusiastic in his work. When he got any new medicine we had all to try it, and Harriet and I were often unwillingly made subjects for his experiments. I remember once, when he was studying the eye, we were made to stand with a full glare of light shining into our eyes while he examined them through an ophthalmoscope. On another occasion I remember we three were alone one evening, and Jack was chasing us round the table trying to pour tea down our throats much against our wills. We had both jumped on chairs to be out of his reach, when the door suddenly opened and one of his fellow-students was ushered in! We all felt decidedly caught, and I do think Jack was a little bit ashamed." The youth who had called for Bowie the student had found Jack the boy. But even in those days, with all their fun and frolic, there was something about him that made his companions feel that Jack Bowie was very true, very reliable,—a fellow they could trust. How diligently and faithfully he worked at college is shown by the places he took in his classes. He was one of the first students of his time. Not every medical student can carry home a gold medal for Physiology, another for Natural History, and a third for the Practice of Medicine, besides numerous other honours. By force of his own ability and diligence he was opening out a career for himself. For a short time he acted as class-assistant to the Professor of Physiology in Edinburgh University, and then he proceeded to Vienna for further study, specially in connection with diseases of the ear and throat. Thereafter, when duly qualified, and with experience enriched by a considerable hospital practice, he went to London to join his brother-in-law, Dr. Potter (now the editor of the *Hospital*), in a large and lucrative practice. From the time he began practice it seemed almost as if the sense of responsibility deepened visibly upon him. In his unremitting devotion to his patients he seemed to carry about with him the burden of anxious cases, and a grave look often shadowed his bright brown eyes. He was an immense favourite with his patients. His quiet, thoughtful, kindly manner inspired confidence, and they trusted him implicitly. In the words of one of them, "his fine eyes looked at one in such a true, friendly, earnest way, that one felt sure this grave doctor would do all he could." In 1886 he married Miss Sara Hankey, daughter of a retired Indian officer, and in a pretty, bright London home they settled happily together. It was a time of sunshine for them—a growing practice, a good income, bright prospects, numerous friends, a happy home. It was in the midst of this sunshine that the call of God came.

During a visit of Mr. and Mrs. D. Clement Scott to this country Dr. Bowie was brought much into contact with the idea of Africa's need, and he began to realise it. The wail of her woes sounded in his ear, and it went to his heart. It seemed to him that there was a splendid field there for medical mission work, and yet medical work seemed to have been rather neglected in all the African Missions. The thought of what such a one as he might do there, with his gift of healing consecrated to God, took hold of him. He thought of the hollowness, the unreality, the hypocrisy of life as he could see it in the great city around him, and a purpose, God-begotten and God-cherished, began to grow in his soul. In many an earnest talk with his like-minded wife it was fostered. We cannot trace the stages of its growth—we would not if we could—but we can understand how deep, how real, was the conviction that grew up within him that God was calling him to go himself; and we can praise God for the day when he saw his way clearly, and was able to write the Convener of the Church of Scotland's Foreign Mission Committee that he was prepared to give up all and go as a medical missionary to Africa, if the Committee would accept him. We can hardly realise what that sentence meant to him when he wrote it. He was no blind enthusiast, carried away by a dream. He knew quite well what he was doing and what it meant. He had counted the cost. The comforts of home, a devoted circle of friends, professional ambition, and the certainty, humanly speaking, of wealth and position—all were his, and deliberately, unostentatiously, devoutly, in penning that sentence he laid them all as a sacrifice on the altar of God. Oh, how small one feels in the presence of such noble self-sacrifice as that! Who of us is worthy to unloose the latchet of its shoes?

And how did the Church accept such a gift, offered at such a cost? It grates upon one's feelings to have to record the Committee's reply, that for want of funds they daren't say that they would accept even such an offer as that! But they would ask the Church; and it is something to be able to tell that within a fortnight the Church replied by subscribing the £2600 required to provide for the cost of his journey out and his modest salary for five years, and Dr. Bowie was told that his noble offer of service for Africa was accepted. There was something very characteristic in his reply. He *thanked* the Committee for accepting him! And he added, "Should it be that I go to Africa, I trust the Church will have no reason to regret her choice." Assuredly she has not, and it is some comfort to-day to know that never for one moment did he regret it either.

I cannot lead you through the experiences of the next two months—busy, trying months for him and his young wife; the breaking up of the pretty home, the parting with the things that had made it so home-like, the preparations for their African life, the hurried "good-byes" to friends. Only those who have gone through it can know what tear-and-wear these mean to a human heart, and how much of it can be compressed into two short months. But all was accomplished, and they sailed from London on the 14th April 1887. As they were just leaving the shores of England he wrote Dr. M'Murtrie, the Foreign Mission Convener, a brief note which showed the current of his thoughts as he went. "There are a number of engineers on board," he said, "going out to Delagoa Bay to lay a railroad. Perhaps in a few years others may be going out to lay one to Blantyre! I hope," he continues, "that by the time I see you again I may have done some useful work for the Church and for Africa." Thus, when the *Hawarden Castle* steamed out into the open sea and the dark night, Jack Bowie on her deck, full of hope and purpose, went forth with God.

Of the voyage out and the journey up the river we have an account from his own pen. Writing of it he says:—" Of our voyage from London to the Cape little can be said, except that it was like other voyages." After describing Cape Town and Natal, he continues:— " At last we reached our seaport, Quilimane, where we arrived on a Sunday afternoon just as the bells were ringing for church. Sara (his wife) certainly was very glad to be finished with the sea and ships. All the way up the coast Sara appeared on deck as we came into port, and disappeared as we left port! We were five or six days at Quilimane getting our boxes safely through the Custom House. Quilimane is a very dull little place, only interesting as being a fair (fair in the sense of *just*) specimen of a Portuguese settlement. It must once have been a place of some little importance, or some inhabitant of it must once have had some energy, for it contains a church built of stones brought all the way from Portugal. The place is Portuguese, and therefore all the business is done by French, Germans, Dutch, Scotch, and East Indians. There is not, so far as I am aware, a single Portuguese house of business except the Custom House.

"... From Quilimane we had to go up the Kwa-Kwa for about eighty miles. This river is in the rainy season a tributary of the Zambezi, but in the dry season there is a mile or two of dry land between them. We went up in a small, open boat like a good-sized ordinary pleasure-boat, with a small box or hut in the centre, where we lived. Our crew consisted of eight black 'boys' or men and a headman called a 'capitan.' This man was supposed to speak and understand English, but of course didn't, so we had considerable difficulty and amusement in making ourselves understood. The journey was really 'roughing it.' For provision for five days we had only some bread, four chickens (about the size of pigeons), some coffee, one-pound tin of salt beef, and some water. Then we had to be all day and all night in our little rabbit-hutch, into which we could just manage to get our two deck-chairs (which, luckily, were comfortable ones), and in these we had to recline all day and sleep all night. Only one of us could get off the chair at a time, and then the unfortunate individual had to kneel on the floor to avoid lifting the roof off. The floor consisted of about eight inches interval between the two chairs. However, we just made a picnic of the thing and enjoyed ourselves. We thought had we been at home such a time would have been considered a delightful adventure, so we just made home there—

and really the river is very picturesque at some parts. For the first day or day and a half the water is very dirty, the banks very muddy, and little to be seen save now and again a crocodile lazily basking in the sun; but after a time the banks become well clothed with vegetation, the water gets clear, and every few miles the stream widens out into a small lake perhaps one or two hundred yards wide, on the shores of which one notices truly tropical vegetation—cocoa-nut palms, Palmyra palms, &c. These little lakes are very beautiful, and when the men come to them they put on a spurt and make the boat jump through the water, the men singing cheerily and not unmusically the while. The mode of progression is somewhat peculiar. The men all sit facing the bow of the boat. Each man has a paddle of wood shaped somewhat like a tennis-racquet, and about the same size. His left hand he places on the end of the handle, while his right grasps the paddle close to the blade; then lifting the paddle vertically and bending forward, he plunges it into the water and pulls it towards him. They try to keep time with the plunge, so that the eight sound as one good plunge.

"On the third day we met a canoe coming down with a letter from Bella (Mrs. Scott), telling us of the death of Mrs. M'Ilwain. This was a great blow, and quite took away all further interest in our journey. The fourth evening we arrived at the end of our Kwa-Kwa journey, and got out of our boat (for the first time since getting in), and crossed to Vicentis, a few huts on the Zambezi, where David, Bella (Mr. and Mrs. Scott), and party were. Here we had to wait five days before the new steamer came and was ready to take us on board. It was a somewhat strange sensation to find ourselves walking out by moonlight, looking down from the high bank on the Zambezi, flowing smoothly past us—strange that it was so little strange! People leave home expecting to come upon marvels, and we are surprised to find that the world is very much alike all round. You might have imagined yourself back two thousand years and looking down upon the Thames from a cluster of huts called London! Our arrival at Vicentis to a small extent helped to lessen the saddening effect of poor Mrs. M'Ilwain's death. We lived in veritable grass huts, dined in a shed, and otherwise rusticated. The women portion ransacked the Company's store (the African Lakes Company have a station at Vicentis) to find wherewith to produce more savoury meals than the poor starved fowl or *nkuku* could afford. In this way they had plenty to do. At last the steamer was ready,—at least everything was ready except that some injector-pipes had to be brazed, and now they found they had no borax wherewith to melt the brass. A trifle this, one would think, but really a serious matter on the Zambezi, many miles from a borax-shop. Fortunately, Sara had brought some borax, which she had intended for a different use, viz., to make my white shirts beautiful, and by much searching we came upon it, and handed it over to braze the pipes. At last everything was ready and everybody on board, and off we went, nobody sorry to leave Vicentis. We had one day and a half on the Zambezi, then branched off into the Shiré, up which we journeyed for seven days, a large portion of the time being spent stuck fast upon sand-banks. It was the first trip of the steamer, and she drew more water than was anticipated, and the river in many parts is very shallow, and—what was worse—nobody seemed to know the channel, so we just went dodging about playing at blind-man's-buff, the channel being the object of search. An hour or so up from Vicentis we landed at Shupanga, and visited Mrs. Livingstone's and Mrs. M'Ilwain's graves. The large baobab-tree under which Dr. Livingstone buried his wife had fallen, its foundations eaten away by white-ants. They had eaten their way about five feet up the inside of the tree, and a high wind coming, it snapped in two. It is not dead, however, and is sprouting again in its fallen position. The whole journey was most picturesque. After entering the Shiré we had hills on our right all the way up, the country between the banks and the hills being finely wooded. Of African monsters, we saw many dozens of hippos, a number of crocodiles, eight or ten elephants, many eagles, and some antelopes.

"We arrived at Katunga's (our landing-place for Blantyre) about four in the afternoon, and at 9.30

next morning started to walk the twenty-nine miles from there to Blantyre, and after undreamt-of labour we reached Blantyre about 8 P.M. the same night. A walk of twenty-nine miles all uphill under an African sun is a labour more enjoyed retrospectively than prospectively. It is something to have accomplished."

Thus the party reached Blantyre, and soon they got settled down to life there. What a changed world that was in which the London doctor now found himself! Everything was changed—life, surroundings, patients, circumstances, appliances—everything except the doctor himself. He was here, in dark Africa, the same quiet, kindly, earnest, attentive, methodical doctor he had been among his London patients. Very soon he became a central feature in the community, and gradually the whole life of the place, native and European alike, became aglow with devotion to him, the key to it all being his own perfect unselfishness in his care for others. Robert Cleland afterwards wrote of him:— "What a splendid man Dr. Bowie is! I could trust my life to him in any circumstances. It is beautiful to see him treat the natives who come to his dispensary every morning with their complaints and sores as kindly and attentively as he would the best lady or gentleman in his practice at home." And what Cleland wrote everybody felt. He had at once settled down to regular methodical work, and very hard work it was. He was a diligent student, regularly devoting several hours a day to study; not only keeping himself abreast of the latest medical science, but keeping up his reading in Greek and German, as well as the current literature of the day. How he did it all, especially in that climate, was a marvel, for no doctor ever devoted himself more assiduously to his patients, whether black or white. A little girl in a London hospital once amused the nurses by giving as a message for the doctor:—" Please, I want the doctor to come and sit down and talk to me." They laughed at her. It was so absurd! Yet that was exactly what Dr. Bowie seemed somehow to find time to do for his patients. One who owed much to his care and skill says:—" He just sat down to talk to you, and he found out in no time what your tastes were and what you cared about. He was a splendid conversationalist, and could talk on any subject. Then he brought you books, which were just of the kind to interest you. He was a perfect circulating library in himself, and his books and his talks and his care over you did as much for you as his drugs." No wonder that the doctor was a man greatly beloved. And yet, with all this, he found time to have leisure which he could spend with the boys, to their great delight and unspeakable good. If you had dropped into his dining-room of an evening, you would probably have found him with a great gathering of boys clustering round him, talking with them, playing with them in their simple native games, making friends with them—all the while winning their young hearts for God. How they loved those evenings! and how they loved the doctor! and how he loved them! "You cannot help getting very fond of the natives," he wrote, "and you cannot help feeling that they are veritably your brother and sister. They are very, very human." He had a dispensary, which was largely attended, but it was not long till he found that an hospital of some sort was a necessity if some of his cases were to be treated successfully at all. With considerable difficulty he got it, and you and I might have smiled at it if we had visited it. Here is his own description of it:—

"We have now got the hospital ready and open. It is a very poor place for what we understand by an hospital, being merely a long mud house of three rooms, with mud floors, and neither beds nor bedding. There are two windows and one door to each room, but in the present rather cold weather these are, in the patients' eyes, a most distinct disadvantage, as the wind blows through the many chinks with anything but pleasing sound to the scantily clothed inmates. However, this is but the first step towards an African St. Bartholomew's, and in Africa before all places one has to 'hasten slowly.' In addition to this mud hospital, we have two other houses in Blantyre entirely devoted to patients. When a sick person comes here to stay he does not come alone. With him comes his mother to cook for him and drive away the flies from his couch. With the mother come the father and brother, uncles and cousins, who cut wood for the fire, smoke, sympathise, and gossip with the sick man and his visitors. Most of these attendants sleep in the same room as the patients, and this very soon fills up a small hospital. It would be very difficult to prevent these people coming and staying, even if we wished to do so, which at present we do not, as we have not yet got an hospital staff to attend to the many needs of the inmates. The question of food is rather a troublesome one, and I think we will soon have to get a regular hospital kitchen and cooks. At present any food except the ordinary native food (which the relatives, if there are any, provide) has to come from our own tables, and our own house-boys have decided and very proper objections to all the soup being portioned to these sick people, and all the fowls to those. We are exceedingly anxious to encourage sick people to come and stay here, as it is by far the best, and indeed the only really good, method of treatment. We are succeeding in our endeavour beyond our hope, and — what is serious—sometimes beyond our means.

"The first patient in our new hospital was a Mandala boy. A gun which he was loading went off and shattered his hand terribly. We had to amputate half his hand, but hope to save a useful thumb and forefinger. He is just a boy, perhaps eighteen years old. For the first two or three days he did nothing but sit rocking himself to and fro, crying for his mother. Now his mother has come, and he is happy."

I wish I could take you round and show you some of his cases. A curious variety you would find them —wounds, bites, burns, sores, besides diseases of all kinds. One case which he had very early on his hands — before he got his hospital — had a peculiar interest at the time, and has a still more pathetic interest now. At the very time when all Europe was thrilled with interest as the most eminent surgeons performed tracheotomy on the Emperor of Germany, Dr. Bowie was performing the same operation on a poor black African woman at Blantyre, and watching with no less solicitude the results of the operation. She had all but died from a cancerous growth in the throat, when the doctor said that if this were tried she might probably live for a year or so longer, and both she and her friends were willing that it should be done — no small tribute to their confidence in the doctor, for the African sorely dreads the knife. With deft and skilful hand the operation was performed and the tube inserted. Soon strength returned, and for twelve months the poor old woman went about breathing through the tube, a marvel to herself and to every one else. But a year soon sped, the numbered months came to an end, and we find the doctor writing:—

"I very much fear our old tracheotomy patient will not live long. It is now just about a year since the operation was performed, and until the last fortnight or three weeks the old woman was very comfortable and well, and able to go about and find for herself. . . . But now she is unable to do anything—even to walk. She lies day and night on a mat in the old store, with all her worldly goods arranged around her. These consist of, first and foremost, her fire, which out here is very often a distinct possession. . . . Around the fire are placed her other goods, a native earthenware pot full of water, with, floating on the top of it, her drinking-cup, a small hollowed-out gourd, and a small basket in which she keeps the food she is unable to eat.

"To a casual observer our old patient would appear a most wretched, dirty, ugly creature. She is old, shrivelled, and wrinkled, her face deformed by the once ornamental scars, her upper lip huge and pendulous, and more disfigured by the hole in which, before her operation, she carried a large *pelele* ring. In addition she has a cataract in her left eye, and when she looks up to you the greyish-green colour of the pupil gives her almost an uncanny look. And yet beneath all this there is a fine human being, and even her face becomes noble to those who have watched her in her long illness. She has struggled bravely on, never complaining, and always most grateful for any attention paid her. Now, poor woman! she is very weak and tired, and has quite lost heart. The other morning, when Nacho and I were down cleaning her tracheotomy tube (this has, of course, to be done daily), she managed to whisper to me, 'Come to me in the forenoon; I want to say something to you.' I asked, 'Can't you say it now?' 'Too many people,' she said. There were two or three other patients close by. We came back again at the time she wanted, and the old woman whispered to me, 'I am very tired; will you give me some medicine to make me die?' It is very sad to see her lying patiently serving her time, especially as nothing can be done to ease her in any way. She has plenty of food, stewed fowls, brandy, milk, and eggs, but she cannot manage to eat much. Her swallowing is very difficult, I fear from extension of the cancer."

This was the way he thought of his patients. So I might take you to many a one to whom he was as an angel of mercy sent from God,—to many a one who, humanly speaking, owed his or her life to the skill and devotion of the brave young doctor during the three years and a half in which he was permitted to serve Africa.

And did he ever regret the change to all this from his London practice? Let him answer for himself. Writing to a relative, he says:—

"Do I regret leaving my cosy house in London, and my comfortable, well-fed patients, to take to a Central African house and unclothed, poorly fed blacks? To which I make answer in Scotch fashion by putting another question, 'Does a slave regret getting his freedom and yearn for his chains once more?' If he does, then he is not free; he is still a slave in all but name. What has my change brought me? I don't know how much; but it has taught me that 'our

America is here, or nowhere;' that one can do God's work anywhere, provided one has the eye to see and the heart to feel—anywhere, I had almost said, better than in a comfortable London practice!"

Oh, how worthless the old had become after he had tasted the joy of the new!

But I must hasten on, and I hardly know how to tell the story of the last days of that noble life. A terrible visitation of influenza had swept over the Mission both in Blantyre itself and in the villages around; natives and Europeans alike were stricken, and more than twenty deaths resulted within a radius of four or five miles. Every one of the Mission staff with one exception was laid down, and very heavy work fell to the doctor. By day in the Mission itself the natives lay on their mats spread on the grass in the open air under the trees, and as he walked through them, stooping to minister to them one by one, he felt, he said, like one walking over a field of battle. The strain upon him, both of fatigue and anxiety, was very great, for he carried the burden of all these patients on his heart, and was unremitting in his attention to them. By-and-by he was himself seized with influenza, and had a very sharp attack. It pulled him down greatly, and he never got up his strength again. In a letter written home when he was just recovering he said:—"We are all needing rest and change,—the very things we cannot get."

It was just on the back of this that there came the

awful ten days. One day Mrs. Henderson's little child was ailing, and Dr. Bowie was asked to come and see him. When he came, he found the little fellow in his bath crowing merrily. He laughed and said, "There's not much the matter with you, old boy." But a little later he came back to examine him. In the course of the examination he looked into the child's mouth, and in a moment there was a change. At the sight which he saw there, a shadow deepened on the doctor's grave face,—a shadow that never lifted, a look that never passed away till the time came when for himself, too, as well as for the child, that day broke when all shadows flee away. Diphtheria was what he saw —and of a very malignant type. All the weary hours of that night he sat by his patient. Hour after hour passed, and the little sufferer grew worse till his sufferings became dreadful to see. By midnight the doctor saw that tracheotomy would be necessary to give even a chance for life, and he determined to perform it whenever daylight came. Oh, how the hearts of these weary watchers wished for the day! Dawn came at last, and the operation was performed. The membrane was far down in the throat, and with terrible determination the doctor sucked the tube again and yet again. The instant sense of relief and the child's grateful, restful look were touching to behold. But to the doctor? Ah! to him this was the breathing of death. Well did he know what it meant. None knew better than he the risk he was running. It was not the first time he had taken his life in his hand thus. More than once before he had done the same both for black patient and white. He wasn't the man to consider himself, or to calculate what risk he ran if he could save a life. He did now just what he had done when the call came to give himself to Africa at the first. He fearlessly did the duty God gave him to do, and left the result with God. The relief which the operation brought was great, but only temporary. The membrane was too far down, and only for twelve short hours was the little life prolonged. At five o'clock the next afternoon the child died. Hardly was the funeral over, the next morning, when Mrs. Henderson lay down, worn out with fatigue and grief. Next day (Friday) the doctor knew that she had diphtheria, and the next he had it himself. Can you think of the consternation which strikes a household here when diphtheria comes to it? What must it have been to the Blantyre household there! But in the midst of the excitement and dread, one man is calm, deliberate, cool. It is Dr. Bowie. From his bed he gives orders to send men away to Mount Milanje (four days' journey) for Dr. W. A. Scott; to send others to Domasi (sixty miles) for Dr. Henry Scott. Then he gives all needed directions as to what should be done by everybody. Regularly from time to time he sent to hear how his sister was, and when he heard that she was worse he rose from his bed and went to see her and do for her whatever could be done.

Sunday came,—and what a Sunday it must have been in that little stricken community! Mrs. Henderson was much worse, and the doctor's strength was greatly reduced, but again he made them help him across from his house to the Manse, that he might see her; and so the weary hours dragged on. Monday morning came, but its daylight brought no cheer. Her sufferings had now become terrible, and again in tracheotomy alone lay the one hope of life. Dr. Harry Scott had arrived from Domasi at four o'clock that morning. He was drenched and weary with his walk of more than sixty miles in fearful rain, which made the journey through the long grass, across the swollen streams and over Mount Ndirande, almost impossible, but he was brave and ready. He had never, however, performed that operation, and in this case there were complications, making it more than usually difficult even for the most experienced surgeon, and Dr. Bowie would not allow him to do it. Bracing himself for the effort, he made them carry him from his own dying-bed to the bedside of his dying sister, and there, with clear head and firm hand, he performed the operation with all his own skill and care, giving immediate and immense relief. It seems so easy to tell all this, but so hard to realise it. We read many a wondrous story of hero and martyr, but surely seldom have we seen anything finer and nobler than the dying surgeon, careless of life, stepping forth to fight death on his own ground. For an hour or two a gleam of hope shone through the cloud, and it almost seemed as if the daring deed were to be rewarded by victory on that desperate field. But the hope was short-lived, for in the afternoon a change for the worse came. After the operation the doctor had been compelled to go home to bed, but by six o'clock she had grown much worse, and sent a message begging him to come to her. Though faint and ill he went at once, and from that time he watched beside her till the end came. She was quite conscious, and knew that she was dying, but she could not speak. They brought her a slate, and she wrote on it dying messages to loved ones far away. Very lovingly "Jack" took them from her one by one as they were rubbed from the slate to make room for others. With a tenderness which those who were present will never forget, he spoke in her dying ear beautiful words of comfort for the darkness of the valley through which he well knew they were both passing. And all the time he never once thought of himself; his whole anxiety was for her.

What a picture of life and love it is that presents itself to us as we look into that African home! We see the brother and the sisters,—those children that long ago played together in the old Edinburgh home,—and we see what God and life and grace have made them. What courage,—what affection,— what Christian confidence,—what triumph over the fear of death! Oh! think of it, Reader, and learn to look reverently on the little children that are playing in the homes of to-day as you wonder what that life may be to which God is calling them.

With Tuesday morning the struggle was over. Poor Harriet passed from her sufferings to her rest, and brave Jack went back to that bed from which, three short days after, he was to follow her home. She had left her messages for home with him, but not to the earthly but to the heavenly home did he carry them. He had been growing steadily worse, and at one time it seemed as if they would have to operate on him too, but the membrane did not extend downwards so as to implicate his breathing, and it was not necessary. His strength, however, rapidly gave way, and on Friday morning the brave doctor, whose short life in Africa had been one record of devoted service, passed away.

If ever a man's life breathed the spirit of Christ, his had done it; and if ever a man died a martyr's brave death, he did. The whole community had been unspeakably distressed before, but when the tidings were told that the beloved doctor was no more, all felt as if their cup of sorrow was full. The news that Dr. Bowie was ill had spread like wildfire through the native villages around, and when word followed that he was dead, a feeling almost of dismay spread through the community. They laid him to sleep in that little Blantyre cemetery, the very dust of which is dear to so many whose eyes have never seen it. The natives had come and asked—touching request!—that they might be allowed to dig his grave. Never had there been in that quiet spot such a gathering as assembled there to lay him to his rest, and there was not, we are told, a dry eye in the mourning crowd. Yet around that grave they sang. With trembling voices, choked by many a sob, they sang his own favourite hymn :—

> "Thou to whom the sick and dying
> Ever came, nor came in vain,
> Still with healing word replying
> To the wearied cry of pain,
> Hear us, Jesus, as we meet,
> Suppliants at Thy mercy-seat."

I shall not attempt to characterise such a life or to estimate its noble work. We bow before it in admiration and awe. Better that we should quietly still our hearts to listen while God Himself speaks to us from it. Like the box of ointment broken whose odour filled the house, such lives poured out fill the land with fragrance and are for the healing of its life.

Of the sorrow in his home I shall not speak, or of the young wife who went forth so bravely, returning to her native land a widow, with her little child orphaned so early. The devoted affection with which the European community outside the Mission regarded him was shown by an immediate request for permission to place in the beautiful new church a series of stained-glass windows in memory of their beloved physician, to whom they owed so much, and whom they had loved so well.

Very deep and solemn, too, was the impression which his death made on the native mind, and tokens are not awanting already that God used that martyr death to perfect and ripen seeds which he had sown during his life. "Except a corn of seed fall into the ground and die, it abideth alone; but if it die, it bringeth forth much fruit."

VI.

Robert Cleland,
THE MISSIONARY OF MILANJE.

REV. ROBERT CLELAND, MISSIONARY, MILANJE.

VI.

ROBERT CLELAND.

IT is no small thing to say of Robert Cleland that he is not unworthy to be named along with two such men as Henry Henderson and John Bowie. He was one with them in spirit, and he was not behind them in courage and devotion. All three had been students of Edinburgh University, Cleland being the last to go forth and the first to be called home. His career was the shortest of the three, but it was long enough to show how deeply "Africa" was written on his heart, and it is not unfitting that with the pioneer missionary who opened the way, and the medical missionary who soothed the sufferings and healed the sickness of the African people, we should link the ordained minister of Jesus Christ who went forth there to teach and to preach the glorious Gospel of the blessed God.

It was neither from the beauties of a rural parish nor from the culture of city life that God called this servant. He came forth to the work of God from a humble home amidst the smoke and dust and noise of Scotland's "Black Country." Born in Coatbridge in 1857, he received his early education first at Dundyvan, and then at Gartsherrie Academy there. After leaving school, he served his apprenticeship as an engineer in one of the large engineering works of which there are so many in that neighbourhood. As a boy he was quiet, painstaking, and in everything very conscientious. I can remember the foreman under whom he served part of "his time" speaking to me years ago of the quiet, industrious lad who never seemed to care for sporting with the other apprentices, but whose mind seemed to be always on his work, always anxious to understand everything about it. Good man! little did he know where the lad's mind really was. That wish to understand everything, too, doubtless made him the "handy" man he was afterwards, able to put his hand to anything—to clean a watch or repair an engine or construct a bridge,—an invaluable gift for such work as lay before him. In the winter evenings he attended the Gartsherrie science classes, where he gained certificates of the Science and Art Department for mathematics, natural philosophy, chemistry, and other branches of science, and this training and the possession of these certificates also proved helpful to him in his future career.

It was in his twenty-first year that he finally decided to give himself to the mission-field. Like Isaiah, he was worshipping in the House of God when the call came to him. It was in the parish church of Garturk, on a Sunday in the late autumn of 1878, and the writer, then a young minister, was making his first missionary appeal to the congregation over which he had been set only a few months before. Looking round the congregation, which included a large number of young men, the preacher asked, "Why should not a congregation like this give not only of its means but of its *men* to the mission-field?" Very earnest was the look that then shone in Cleland's face. It was as if his very soul was gazing out of those deep, dark eyes of his. He seemed to hear the voice of God saying, "Whom shall I send? and who will go for us?" and reverently he answered, in his heart, "Here am I! Send me." From that hour he was consecrated to God and to Africa. Much and often did he pray over it, but from that decision he never swerved or turned back. With characteristic reticence he buried his secret in his bosom for months. No one heard from him one single word telling of the new purpose that filled his soul, but all the time he was busy preparing for the work to which he had devoted himself. He determined to qualify himself for the position of an Ordained Minister, and his first step was to begin toiling away quietly by himself at his Latin and Greek. His fellow-workmen used afterwards to tell how he brought his Greek Grammar with him to his work, and how, when the dinner-hour came and the others went home to dinner, he would sit in a corner of the shed eating his "piece" and getting up his Greek verbs. At length the time came when his secret must come out, or so much of it, at least. One day he called for me and, to my surprise, asked if I would examine him in Latin and Greek to see whether I thought him fit for entering college. As was to be expected, his knowledge of these subjects was comparatively meagre, but the offer of a little "coaching" during the week or two that remained ere the opening of the college session was gratefully accepted, and the progress of these few weeks showed what a power of work he possessed.

In due time he entered the University of Edinburgh, and there, in face of difficulties that would have daunted a less determined spirit, he worked his way through the full seven years of a university course, helping at the same time to maintain himself by teaching. He worked very hard, studying late and early. No one knew how much it cost him to make up all the leeway of those years, and to keep up with classfellows who had been taught and drilled in classics at school and then gone straight to college. In all his classes he acquitted himself creditably, gaining the approval of his professors and the respect and regard of his fellow-students. For a short period after his first college session was ended he went to Lancaster. Here it was that his Science and Art Department certificates stood him in stead, for it was by the help of these that he obtained an appointment as a teacher of science in Lancaster Commercial School. He greatly enjoyed his time there, and in after-years he looked back gratefully to the experience he had gained while thus engaged, and to the friendships which he had formed there. In due time he returned to college and resumed his hard and steady work. During several winters he taught for some hours every evening the boys residing in the Home of the Edinburgh Industrial Brigade. It was congenial work, but it was very hard. The big lads, sometimes rough, though not unkindly, felt the influence of his strong personality and devotion to them, and they liked him. But it was no light thing to keep them occupied and busy with their work through a whole winter evening, and when at ten o'clock he left them and walked wearily home to his lodgings, he was often much more fit for going to bed than for sitting down, as he regularly did, to pore over his own studies till the small hours of the morning. Yet he never flinched, and the thought of giving it up or turning back never once crossed his mind. In the summer of 1886 he went for some months to be missionary at Achnacarry, in Lochaber, under the late Dr. Archibald Clark of Kilmallie, and kindly recollections of him still linger among the people there. When visiting in that locality recently, I was struck with the affectionate way in which some of the people I met still spoke of him. The tremble in the voice and the eyes that filled as they spoke told of the strong tie with which there, as everywhere, he seemed to attach people to him. He was very happy in his work in Lochaber. There was something about the great hills and the quiet glens that appealed to him, and he loved tramping about among them—those great long walks he had to take preaching and visiting his people. It was like a foretaste of his future work, and left its impression upon him. Twelve months later, when, in his first letter home, he was describing his approach to Blantyre, he wrote:—"For miles we were passing through a steep, hilly country, prettily wooded, so like Clunes Hill in Lochaber that sometimes I could almost believe that time was a year rolled back."

All this time he was dreaming of Africa with an enthusiasm that was almost a passion. Eagerly he read every book that could give him information about it. But Livingstone was his great ideal. More than one pilgrimage did he make from his home at Old Monkland over to Blantyre to visit the birthplace of his hero and see the mills where he had worked as a boy and the scenes amidst which he had been reared. That a double portion of that master's spirit might rest upon him was the constant prayer of his eager youthful heart. Every step of the great traveller's journeys through the Dark Continent he had traced again and again, and every station in the African mission-field he knew. At that time it seemed as if there was no prospect of his being sent to Africa by his own Church. The funds at the disposal of the Foreign Mission Committee, and responsibilities already resting upon them, greater than they could meet, forbade their increasing the staff of missionaries in the African field; but he laboured on in his preparation, assured that God would open a way for him when the time came that he was ready to go. And so He did. Cleland's last session at college was within a few weeks of being ended when an unexpected call came for a missionary to go to Africa. The Rev. David Clement Scott, head of the Blantyre Mission, had been home on furlough after five years of work in Africa, and by his fervid enthusiasm and stirring words had kindled a flame of sympathy for African Missions in many hearts. One point which he had repeatedly and strongly urged was the importance of strengthening the Mission by opening a new station at Mount Milanje, an important centre and the residence of a powerful chief, about four days' journey from Blanytre. The old difficulty, however—want of money—stood in the way, and Mr. Scott, at the close of his furlough, had to sail again for Africa without having obtained the additional missionary he desired. His words of appeal, however, remained behind him like seeds taking root in Christian hearts, and long before he reached Blantyre their fruit began to appear. A few friends in the congregation of St. George's Church, Edinburgh, impressed by the necessity and the opportunity, offered to bear the expense of sending out a missionary if one could be sent at once.

Shortly after this, there was a gathering of students in the rooms of the Church, 22 Queen Street, and Dr Scott, minister of St. George's, who was present chanced in the most casual way to meet Cleland among others, and made his acquaintance. It was not long before he discovered where the lad's heart was and what was the desire of his life. Subsequent inquiries abundantly satisfied him that here was just the kind of man that was needed for Milanje, and for which he and his friends were looking. The result was, that, after careful consideration by the Foreign Mission Committee, the appointment was offered to Cleland. Surely no one called to leave his native land ever received the summons with more eager joy. He wrote to his mother a characteristic letter, and on getting back her willing consent,—written with characteristic solemnity and reverence,—he accepted the appointment. One hardly knows whether to admire more the mother lovingly yielding her son to God for such work, or the son going forth in such a spirit. "Of course, I am grateful for the appointment," he wrote to the Secretary of the Foreign Mission Committee, "and I trust that a devoted life may reveal my sincerity of heart better than any mere words can do." He was licensed to preach the Gospel by the Presbytery of Edinburgh in April 1887, and on the 29th May following he was ordained a Missionary to Africa in St. George's Church, Edinburgh. It was during the sittings of the General Assembly, and there was a crowded congregation, among whom were many ministers and others from all parts of the country. To him, with his shrinking, sensitive nature, it was a terribly trying occasion. "I would rather cross Africa," he wrote to a friend, "than face the awful ordeal. It seems a shame to put a poor broken-down mortal through such a public trial, but I suppose the feelings of the one must be sacrificed that those of the many may be touched. This seems to be the law of all true life." Certainly, as he stood there the centre of the great gathering, so pale and earnest-looking, and yet so calm and self-possessed, with the gentle light shining in his dark eye, there was something that drew the sympathies of all hearts to him, and a link of personal sympathy was forged which made many a one watch with prayerful interest the steps of his subsequent career. At the close of the service hundreds thronged round him eager to shake hands with the young missionary and bid him "God-speed," among them being a number of boys and girls, for each of whom he had a personal word, which no doubt they would long remember. His mother was prevented by illness from going to Edinburgh to be present at his ordination, and he had only a few days in which to go home to Old Monkland and see her before he left. Busy days they were, full of preparations and hurried farewells to old friends and companions. Then he paid a flying visit to Leeds on his way south,— to say "good-bye" to a brother who was there,—and then on to London, all within the week. Here, too, he had a busy time—so many places to go and so many things to be got, so many instructions to be attended to, and withal so little time to think, so little opportunity for the pent-up fountain of feeling to find outlet. When he went on board the *Roslin Castle* he met another young missionary also on his way to his first work in the African field, Mr. W. Bell, an engineer, who was going out to Mandala in the service of the African Lakes Company. At once the two took to each other, and during the long voyage the companionship and communion of a kindred spirit was very helpful to both. The vessel sailed from London on the 9th June. I was one of those who stood and saw him wave his last farewell as the *Roslin Castle* steamed out of the dock, and a bright farewell it was, without one trace of sorrow or regret. Even in that hour of parting from home and kindred, a bright joy lit his face at the thought that Africa and his work there for God were now so near. After watching till the little group of friends on the pier-head had faded in the distance behind, the two young missionaries sat down and had a long, earnest talk about the work to which they were going, and it drew them very close together, that talk. Then Cleland went below to write, and as the vessel was steaming out of the Thames he wrote to his most intimate college friend, and this was how his letter began:—

"Bound for Africa at last!—the land of my hopes, and, I trust, sooner or later (it may sound strange), the land of my grave! Oh, to live for it and die for it! and to lie there with all the seeds of your work growing up around you until we rise to meet *Him!*

I always like to think of sleeping my long sleep in one of those vast solitudes—solitudes in which the wail of the slave now rises to heaven, but which one day will be a garden of God."

To another friend he wrote at the same time :—

"It is not simply that I am leaving for Africa. That never gives me a thought—except the thought, Am I worthy for work in Africa? Will I be able, with the help of a Higher Hand, to do something for Africa? . . . May He who sustains all and is over all prepare me, soul and body, for the Master's use! The great ideal of my life has been to do something for Africa, even if it should be His will that I only take possession of the land by a grave. Oh that, in the truest sense, I may be consecrated for such a work! Africa has been the dream of my past, and God's leading encourages me to believe that it will be the joy of my future. It is among my dearest wishes to be at last laid in its solitudes as a *finger-post* to point the way for others. I may fall, but I will as certainly rise again."

Sadly prophetic words! How we read them now! And how soon have they been fulfilled! They were not like the ordinary words of a student writing to his chums. They were a revelation of the man himself, and showed what manner of man he was and in what spirit he went forth. "Africa" was written on his heart. To do something for poor suffering Africa was the dream of his life, and no sacrifice did he think too great, not even life itself, if he could thereby help in healing "this open sore of the world." Surely it was God who implanted that burning desire in his soul! And to think that already his work for Africa is over, after only three short years and a half! To-day there is sorrow in the old home, sorrow among the missionary band at Blantyre, sorrow in the Church; but Cleland has got his wish. God gave him his desire. He worked for Africa; he died for Africa; and now he is sleeping his long sleep in one of those vast solitudes, and the seeds of his work are growing, and will grow up around him until the day when he shall rise to meet *Him*.

Of his voyage out little need be said. It, too, was like other voyages. He greatly enjoyed it, and was much benefited in health by the rest and the sea-breezes. He had a great regard for the captain of the ship, and spoke most gratefully of much personal kindness which he had received from him. Changing his steamer at the Cape, he found sailing up the east coast rather tiresome, and was not sorry when they anchored off Quilimane. Here the first shadow fell on his path. Tidings met him there of the death of poor Mrs. M'Ilwain, who had died at Vicentis as the Mission party preceding him went up the river. After two days at Quilimane, he, with a fellow-traveller as a companion, started at midnight in a small boat for Vicentis, on the Zambezi, under conditions which reduced the comforts of travelling to a minimum. "We slept," he says, "in a little grass house in the boat, about three feet high and four feet wide. At our heads were the bare legs of the native steersman; at our feet (mine reached far out of the house) were the rowers, singing their musical chant as they pulled together at the oars." Three days of this, followed by two and a half days' march through the long grass under a burning sun, brought them to Vicentis, the heat during the latter part of the march being very trying. Writing of it long after, he said he had never felt it so hot as he had done that day. At Vicentis he expected to get the African Lakes Company's steamer up the River Shiré, but on his arrival he learned that the steamer would not arrive for a week yet. Vicentis is a cheerless and unhealthy spot on the river-bank, and very reluctantly he waited there. The end of the long week came, but not yet the steamer. A day or two later came Lieutenant Wissmann, who had just crossed the continent, taking four years to the task. He had passed through Blantyre, and gave a glowing account of the place; but he also brought word that it would probably be a fortnight yet ere the steamer could arrive. Two or three days longer Cleland waited, and then, as there seemed no prospect of the steamer, he started in a small boat with a crew of ten men, not one of whom knew a word of English,—which, he says, not unreasonably, he found "a great disadvantage!" The slow, weary progress of a passage up the river in one of these boats has often been described—the high banks, and the mud, and the rank smell of the decaying vegetation, and the heat, and the discomforts of the boat, and the irregularity of meals, and the chance character of the food that one could prepare for himself when the men stopped to cook their own food. One does not wonder that, in the midst of these, the fever-tyrant had his hand on him before he reached Blantyre. "On my fourth day out," he says, "I had an attack of what *I call* 'bilious fever.' It lasted a little more than four days, after which, however, I was able to take to shooting hippos." Some time later, however, he writes:—"My health here (at Blantyre) has been quite as good as at home, but they say that my 'bilious attack' on the river was fever, and in the circumstances I dare say I could hardly fail to have been saturated with malaria."

Eleven days after leaving Vicentis he reached Katungas, the landing-place for Blantyre, from which it is twenty-nine miles distant, and here he inserts a characteristic parenthesis:—"By the way, Katunga is the Makololo chief, and was one of Livingstone's 'boys.' Strange that so many of the river chiefs were Livingstone's men, who seem to have risen by force of character to what they are!"

The march up the road from Katungas was speedily accomplished, and about 9 P.M. in the evening he reached Blantyre, Mr. Scott and Mr. Duncan having walked out some miles to meet him. Like all who go to Blantyre, he fell in love with it at first sight.

His expectations of it were high. "Every white man I met between this and Quilimane," he wrote, "had said to me, 'But wait till you see Blantyre!'" But, high as they were, these expectations were more than fulfilled, and he wrote home a glowing description of the place, the work, the people, and, above all, of his own kindly reception among them. "Even the little black boys and girls," he said, "came peeping into the room to see the new minister."

"I wish you could see Blantyre," he wrote again; "you cannot conceive how much good it is doing to Africa. Boys are here trained to all kinds of work, and many of them are deeply pious. In a few years these will spread through the land. Even the natives who pass through here daily with their spears, bows and arrows, and guns are being silently influenced for good. You cannot expect with a race like these such results as some good people at home are tired looking for, but one realises here that day by day a change is being wrought on the whole country round about."

At once he fell into line and took his place in the work of the Mission. That gift he had of winning the affection of all who knew him well soon endeared him to his colleagues, and his stay at Blantyre was a busy and happy time. But the post for which he was destined was Mount Milanje, a mountain district about fifty miles from Blantyre, on the very edge of the Shiré Highlands. Here Mr. Scott, the head of the Mission, had long desired to plant a station. It was not only an important native centre, but it was also a place where the Arabs were in great numbers, and from which caravans of slaves were continually being sent to the coast. It was, further, as Cleland said, *the key to Quilimane*, as, in the event of the river being at any time blocked by war, Milanje commanded the direct line of the overland route to the coast. But Milanje was ruled by a powerful chief, Chikumbu, who was unfriendly to the Mission. He had an old-standing grievance as to some runaway slaves of his, Chipetas, having been harboured at Blantyre years before. The first step, therefore, was to visit Chikumbu and secure, if possible, friendly relations with him. Accordingly Mr. Scott, accompanied by Mr. Duncan, set off on a journey to Milanje for this purpose. Arrived at Chikumbu's after their fifty miles' walk, they found that the chief refused to see them personally. For two days they were kept waiting to learn his decision as to the reception which should be given them, and one can understand the anxiety of two such days, waiting on the whim of a powerful and treacherous chief whose cross mood or fretful temper might at any time utter the word which would mean their death. But their hope was in God. After two days, Chikumbu, who still refused to see them, sent his headmen to demand the immediate return of his slaves. Mr. Scott met this demand with a counter-proposal that he would redeem the men, purchasing their freedom at thirty-two yards of calico per head. This proposal was at once rejected by the headmen with sundry threatenings and war-like demonstrations, and with a disappointed heart, but grateful to the Providence that had spared their lives, Mr. Scott and Mr. Duncan returned to Blantyre.

Baffled thus for a time at Milanje, Cleland went to Chirazulo,—a place fifteen miles from Blantyre, on the way to Domasi,—and founded a Mission station there. Here settling among a people who welcomed his coming among them, he erected with his own hands, aided only by native help, a building for a church and school and a house for himself, making roads, building bridges, laying out a garden and fields, as well as establishing a school and teaching the natives, preaching all the while both by life and lips the Gospel of Jesus Christ. Here he laboured for nearly three years,—a true pioneer, with heart and head and hand all disciplined and ready for whatever God might give him to do. For a great part of that time he was there alone, with never a white man for a companion. It was a lonely post, but he loved the African people with a wonderful devotion. "You would love them too," he wrote, "if you only knew them." He saw much of the horrors of the slave-trade, and often his heart bled for the wrongs and sufferings which he saw inflicted. More than once with his own money he redeemed the slave, and with his own hand sawed the slave-stick from the neck and set the captive free. Again and again, in his loneliness, he was down with the terrible fever, but ever as he recovered he was at work again. One of his letters, written from Chirazulo on the 27th October 1888, gives some idea of the heart-pressure under which that work was carried on by the lonely missionary :—

"Work here," he says, "continues as usual. We cannot boast, but I do pray that some seed may fall on good ground; and I know it will. Yesterday we went to the hill in the morning as usual. Just fancy yourself in Africa on a mountain side. The sun is shining brightly on the native village, with its beehive-like grass huts. Here and there under huge trees are gathered groups of people. On a rock near, women are pounding maize, men are weaving mats, and the children are happy at play. A little way apart from one of these groups, and alone, we see a slave sitting painfully under the weight of a heavy slave-stick. His eyes are dreamily following us. We speak to a group of women, and they ask us when rain will come. 'Father,' they say, 'pray for rain, or there will be hunger.' After conversing with groups here and there, and asking them to come to the 'talk about God,' we get all gathered under one village tree. Just as the service is beginning we hear far away up on the hillside a woman calling with that peculiar strained voice—strained to suit the distance. All is silence. Then we hear again, and this time we distinguish plainly the word *ngondo*, and soon several of the men rush up. It is news of war. Some boys from the other side of the hill have been captured at Lake Shirwa when fishing with their fathers. All is excitement, and we hear them say, 'They will be taken to the Matapwiri,'—a great Arab centre on Milanje, whence they will be driven to the coast, sold, and perhaps shipped off who knows where? In a little some one suggests, 'Let us be quiet until the white man speaks about God, and then we will hear about the war.'" . . . Writing at another time he says :—" At the service in church here we had about a hundred people present, but no children. The mothers, I heard, were afraid, and kept them at home. One of those present was a slave whose future was very uncertain. A more touching scene could not be depicted than when he stood alone outside our little church, with no one to take up the burden of his heavy yoke, and so help him on; or as he sat on the ground behind the rest, so wretched-looking, painfully twisting his neck in the slave-stick to look up or around him. But what is this case, heartrending though it be, to that of the thousands who are herded down that dreadful way to the coast at Shirwa? I found I was on a great slave-route, and saw a caravan said to be with ivory. 'Yes,' said one of my boys, 'but black ivory!' . . . That poor slave I spoke of has begged me to buy him. 'I may be sold to the coast soon,' he said. 'Buy me, and I will do your work.' His poor heart is breaking, but his is only one in a multitude of breaking hearts in this dark land. I shall never forget how one day a poor woman rushed into the station and cried for me—for the white man—to save her. 'They are taking me to the coast to sell me,' she said.

'Oh, save me! They have stolen me from my home with the Chikumbu tribe over the river.' I often wonder where she is now. Perhaps her heart broke altogether on that dark way to the coast, or is breaking now, somewhere far away, for her old home over the river. People at home cannot, I think, feel as we feel when we stand face to face—ay, and often helpless—before such scenes. But with life before us hope runs high, and we thank God in our loneliness for the great blessedness of being able to do our weak little best to bind up the broken-hearted, to proclaim liberty to the captives and the great brotherhood of men. Oh, come over and help us!"

With that strange, deep love of Africa filling his soul, everything about its poor degraded suffering life seemed to go to his very heart. In another letter he wrote:—" How touching it was to hear, through the grass walls of the hut where I slept, a woman wailing for hours for her husband, who had long been dead! She had dreamed of him in the night, and (as is the custom) she came out and paced before her hut through the silent hours of the morning, calling him to come back to her in strangely pathetic and yet weirdly musical words, pausing at times to speak to the dead in her natural voice." But, indeed, never a letter came from him in which he did not sigh over the cruel wrongs of his adopted people; and how his indignation flashed when he thought of self-satisfied Christians in the Church at home supinely indifferent to these things, callous to such sufferings, and deaf to every appeal on their behalf! He could not understand such people.

In the autumn of 1888 the Rev. Alexander Hetherwick, missionary at Domasi, a station fifty-five miles north-east of Blantyre, came home on a much-needed and well-earned furlough, and during the sixteen months he was absent Cleland took charge of the work at Domasi, along with his own work at Chirazulo, walking regularly the long distance between the two places. There he had the companionship of Mr. R. S. Hynde, teacher of the Mission school. The companionship of such a one was a great joy to him, and a fast friendship was formed between the two. It was no mere formal supervision of the work that he took while at Domasi. It was like everything he did, thorough and laborious. Nor was it confined to preaching and teaching. He was as ready with the spade and the hammer and the axe as he was with the Yao lesson-book or the New Testament. At the time of Mr. Hetherwick's return we read in the *Blantyre Supplement*—the little magazine printed at the Mission printing-press :—

"Mr. Cleland has done Roman work here during the sixteen months of Mr. Hetherwick's absence. A footpath eight miles in length has been hoed along the base of Mount Zomba from Mr. Buchanan's plantations to the station at Domasi, and has facilitated immensely communication between the two places.

Mr. Buchanan cleared part of it at his end as far as the boundary of his property on the Naisi. A good road has been made from the station to the chief's village, crossing the Domasi River by a bridge which is a triumph of engineering skill. A water-channel fully a mile long brings the water of the Chifunde stream close to the station—a great boon. Thus we have good roads and good water,—two potent civilizers of a new country."

Then he returned to Chirazulo and continued the work there, not without encouraging tokens of blessing. To help him in it he had with him Kapito and his wife, Rondau,—natives who had been in the Mission at Blantyre ever since its commencement. They had been baptized a few years before, and on Easter Sunday 1887 they had sat down together at the Table of Holy Communion, the first communicants of the native Christian Church. Now they are helping to train their countrymen in the knowledge and love of Christ, and faithfully and happily Cleland and they lived and worked together. From time to time he paid short visits to Blantyre, where he was always a welcome visitor, and occasionally he preached in the church there. This was always a trial to him, for he was terribly diffident of his own powers; but some of those who were accustomed to hear him, speak of his remarkable power in the pulpit, of his singularly clear perception of the truth, and of the spiritual power with which he preached.

But Milanje was his destination, and he never lost sight of that goal. All this time he was looking across to the mountain as the place where he was yet to be, and repeated journeys thither had been undertaken in hope of finding the door open for starting the Mission there. After the visit of Mr. Scott and Mr. Duncan, already referred to, and while they were returning to Blantyre disappointed at Chikumbu's refusal to make terms of friendship, the chief changed his mind, or perhaps he took a different view of the situation from his headmen. Perhaps it occurred to him to ask himself whether all those yards of calico should be lost, or whether it might not be dangerous to offend "the white man." However it might be, he sent his son to Blantyre with a diplomatically polite message. He was sorry that, having been away on a hunting expedition, he had not seen Mr. Scott (!), but he hoped he would soon return to visit him, when he was sure some amicable terms could be arranged. Some time after, Mr. Scott paid a second visit, accompanied by Dr. Bowie, and saw the formidable chief in his native village, when they were able to settle the matter of the slaves and their redemption, and to establish friendly relations between him and the missionaries. A formal document was prepared, and duly signed by the various parties to the agreement. It is something of a curiosity in its way. It is as follows :—

"BLANTYRE, QUILIMANE, EAST AFRICA,
26th May 1888.

"By these presents be it known that I, the headman of Chikumbu, have received on Chikumbu's behoof, to carry to Chikumbu from Mr. Scott, head of the Blantyre Mission, on behoof of said Mission, two trusses of cloth, and that this is the earnest to Chikumbu himself of three more trusses yet to follow· to be divided amongst Chikumbu's headmen as Chikumbu himself shall see fit, and that these five trusses shall be for settlement of all past *mlandu* concerning slaves and all else, and the establishment of friendly relations between the English and the said chief, Chikumbu.

"In witness of which first part of transmission to said Chikumbu, we, the undersigned, append our signatures.

  (Signed) JOHN BOWIE.
        DAVID CLEMENT SCOTT.
        MASONGA (his mark).
        D. C. S., *Witness.*
        CHENDOMBO (his mark).
        D. C. S."

"BLANTYRE, 4th *June* 1888.

"Be it further known that three trusses of calico are this day handed over to Chikumbu's headman, Masonga, and headman Kanjole with him, on behoof of Chief Chikumbu; and that Chikumbu through them now declares that these five trusses (viz., the two formerly sent and these present three) finish the *mlandu*; that there is no further ground of quarrel between the Chief Chikumbu and the English on account of slaves which formerly ran away, or on account of any one of the slaves; and that friendship is herewith established and secured.

"In witness whereof, we, the undersigned, set to and append our names.

    (Signed)   DAVID CLEMENT SCOTT.
            MASONGA (his mark).
            KANJOLE (his mark).
            JOHN BOWIE.
            DOUGLAS R. PELLY.
            HENRY HENDERSON.

"Signed this fourth day of June, eighteen hundred and eighty-eight years, at Blantyre Mission Station, Shiré Hills, East Africa."

Such were the title-deeds to Milanje. They opened its closed door, and the chief now expressed his desire that the missionaries would come and live in his territory. How gladly would Cleland have gone! But by that time it was impossible, for Hetherwick was away home, and he had Domasi on his hands as well as Chirazulo. There were other difficulties in the way, too. Chikumbu himself was fickle and uncertain, although when, at Christmas-time (1888), Cleland paid a visit to the mountain, he still desired him to come and live there. Portuguese troubles, too, were now hanging over the Mission, hindering everything and increasing the difficulties and uncertainty, and it was not till May 1890 that Cleland was able to go to Milanje definitely to settle. Chikumbu received him with every token of friendship, and both the Wayao and their neighbours, the Wanyasa, under Chipoka, welcomed him; but it was not long before it became evident that Chikumbu's friendship was not to be depended on. Cleland's tent was pitched under the great trees on the side of the mountain, and he desired to purchase land on which to erect a house. So many difficulties and troubles however, were raised regarding the land, that Cleland's carriers, who had brought his things, began to suspect the chief of seeking a quarrel which might furnish an excuse for seizing the goods, and it was with difficulty that they were prevented from running away in the night. Several days full of anxiety and trouble were thus spent, when, to make matters worse, Cleland was laid down with fever. After a few miserable days he was sufficiently recovered to go off, leaving tent and everything, and make a hurried journey to Blantyre. Here he got quit of his fever, and after a few days more, was able to return to Milanje, Mr. M'Ilwain, the joiner, accompanying him. Soon things seemed satisfactorily settled, and Mr. M'Ilwain was able to return to Blantyre, leaving Cleland to the work of clearing the ground and preparing the sun-dried bricks for the erection of a schoolhouse and of establishing the Mission by opening a school for the Wayao children.

And so he was on Mount Milanje at last! Oh, the joy it was to him to be there! I wish I could let you see the eager, happy missionary at his work,—his little tent under the great trees, and himself and his co-workers busy as could be, making bricks, digging foundations, teaching the children. In the September number of the *Blantyre Supplement* he wrote:—" After more than ten years of effort the Mission has at last secured a footing on Mount Milanje!" The goal of his hopes was reached. The standard of the Cross was planted on those heights which he had been sent out to claim, and his heart rejoiced.

For a time things went smoothly, but his difficulties were not yet over. They were in reality only beginning. The two tribes which were to unite in peace around the missionaries of the Prince of Peace were still savages, and they could not easily throw aside their wild nature. Chikumbu, who had been for years the scourge and terror of his district, was still eager to have the Wanyasa people under his rule, and treachery and cruelty, war and bloodshed, soon broke out around the young Mission. One day Chikumbu made a sudden and fierce attack on the weaker tribe, the chief himself at the head of his warriors wildly waving an Arab flag inscribed with verses from the Koran, and urging on the slaughter and destruction. Cleland, who was at the time suffering from fever, hurried to the scene, and heedless of risk or danger, made his way through the fight to the chief, and quietly but firmly taking the flag from his hand, ordered him to desist. Strangely impressed, the chief submitted, and yielded up his flag, saying, "Lalal (Cleland) has a brave heart, like Chikumbu himself." For a time the fighting was over, but the feud was deep-seated and chronic, and Chikumbu was grasping and treacherous, and again and again trouble and difficulty arose. At one time Cleland thought of removing to some more peaceful part of the mountain, but to do that was to leave the Wanyasa to the tender mercies of Chikumbu, so he held on at his trying post. His faith failed not, and his work went on. "Our small school, since started," he wrote, "will, we trust, not be hindered by future hostilities, and we hope that the difficulties of these last three months may be but the birth-throes of a future day of peace, when the healing beams of the Sun of Righteousness will kindle the love of man to man in the dear love of God."

Early in September he went to Blantyre to attend a meeting of the Missionary Council, when his friends wrote that, in spite of the troubles he had gone through, he was looking much better than when he was there before. He was so bright and happy, and seemed altogether in such good spirits, though his troubles were by no means over, and it was settled that Dr. W. A. Scott should accompany him on his return, to support him in any further difficulties with Chikumbu. Sunday the 14th September was Communion Sunday at Blantyre. In the morning they all sat together at the Table of the Lord, and in the evening Cleland preached and closed the Communion service. Very beautiful,—almost like a vision,—is the glimpse we get of the little church that day, and the little company of disciples, for so many of whom it was the last Communion on earth. I love to think of Cleland closing that memorable service, so far away from the Coatbridge smoke,—so far from the green hills of Lochaber,—in the heart of suffering Africa, which he loved so passionately, yet in the bosom of the Christian church planted there through Christian sacrifice,—in that fellowship of the saints which was so sweet to him, and in the very holy of holies of the Christian temple, standing himself with uplifted hands speaking words of benediction on the Church of God. It was from such a time of Holy Communion that he went out again into the night, as his Master went to the garden and the Cross.

There is not much more to tell—only the end. Dr. W. Scott and he returned to Milanje, but the difficulties with Chikumbu increased to such an extent that they were relunctantly obliged to leave him, for a season at least. They made a journey down the Ruo, and then returned to a place at the Linge, between Chikumbu's and Nkanda's. After spending a few days with a headman, Chakamonde, they went into a little round native hut near the place they had chosen for their new quarters. There they remained for a week, during which time Cleland went across to Chikumbu's and had "the stuff" brought over. Then they set to work to prepare a new station, Dr. Scott digging pits for the poles of the schoolhouse, and Cleland working at a bit of a road to the stream. That afternoon (Tuesday) Cleland took ill—very ill. Both of them had been having touches of fever, off and on, for some time; but this was much more serious. What a blessing it was and how thankful we are now that his companion at the time was the doctor! Everything was done that could be, but there was no improvement. He grew worse. On Thursday messengers were despatched to Blantyre for more medicines and port wine, and the doctor had him moved a great way up the hill, near the rocks. By this time he was completely prostrate. It was a terrible place for wind up there near the hilltop, so Dr. Scott had a little house built, nine feet by twelve, high in the centre, and strong, with a grass roof, and "tolerably cosy." All Friday and Saturday he lay there, every symptom growing alarmingly worse, till the doctor had almost lost hope. He was dull and apathetic and not like himself, "which," says Dr. Scott, "made one feel it was *a patient* he was attending, and not poor Cleland, which was somewhat easier to do." On Saturday the messengers returned from Blantyre, bringing a *machilah* to convey him thither. He was himself anxious to go, so next morning men were got for carriers,—fortunately without much difficulty—and the party set out for Blantyre as fast as it was possible to go. That night they stopped to rest at a place called Medima, a weird, dreary place. Dr. Scott, writing of it, says:— "I would rather have gone on to Chintzorbedzi, for Medima is a doleful place. It is the place where that Japanese died; and there is another grave, too; and lions infest the place. Cleland, however, wished to stop there, and we did so. It was a strange, strange night. At midnight he was so ill I scarce thought he could live through it, and I said to myself, 'If not to-night, it will be to-morrow night.' The hiccough was constant now, rhythmical, every third inspiration; and what a sound it made there—without another in all the lonely forest except now and again a leopard grunting round the camp." After resting till 2.40 A.M. the caravan started again. It was pitch-dark, and they had to pick their way through the bush by the light of the candle-lantern which Dr. Scott carried, who, poor man! worn with fatigue and watching, was sleeping on his feet as he walked, and from time to time stumbled into the bush as the path took a sharp or sudden turn. A dreary sunrise saw them eagerly pushing on, and at 10.30 the sad procession filed into Blantyre, twenty-four hours and a half from the time they had left the mountain.

Arrived there, remedies were applied and everything that love and skill and care could do for him was done. The sight of friends around him, and especially of his beloved Dr. Bowie, acted like a tonic. He brightened up on seeing them. "It does me good to see you," he said to Dr. Bowie; and he really seemed to improve. Alas! it was the flickering before the darkness. Dr. Bowie and Mr. Scott arranged to divide the night between them to watch by him by turns, but in the first watch of the night, about ten o'clock, while Mr. Scott was with him, without a word, without a struggle, he passed away. His warfare accomplished, his toils over, another "Livingstone Man" had died for the redemption of Africa. As they looked on him there, so peacefully at rest after all his labours, a feeling almost of envy was in every heart,—"*Blessed are the dead which die in the Lord from henceforth: Yea, saith the Spirit, that they may rest from their labours; and their works do follow them.*"

This was the 10th of November. Next day they laid him in the little cemetery at Blantyre, natives and Europeans sorrowing together around his grave. Thus Cleland of Milanje sleeps his long sleep, as he prayed that he might, in one of the vast solitudes, and already the fruits of his work are growing up around him. Already those vast solitudes are becoming the garden of God.

> "Now the labourer's task is o'er,
>   Now the battle-day is past,
> Now upon the farther shore
>   Lands the voyager at last.
> Father, in Thy gracious keeping
> Leave we now Thy servant sleeping."

Very deep was the impression made at home by the news of the young missionary's death,—and especially among those who, like himself, were still young men. He had been one of the earliest members of the Church of Scotland Young Men's Guild—a Union embracing a large proportion of the young men of the Church. He had been the first to go from its ranks to the mission-field; and he was the first of their number to be laid in a missionary's grave. We do not wonder, therefore, that when the Guild first met in its Annual Conference after his death, the Delegates present, representing their brethren in all parts of the land, resolved to erect in the new church at Blantyre a Memorial Tablet recording their affectionate remembrance of him and his work. And so, beside the tablet that there commemorates Henry Henderson, and the windows that speak of Dr. Bowie, there is to be seen a simple brass tablet bearing the following inscription :—

THE REV. ROBERT CLELAND,
Born at Coatbridge, Scotland, September 4, 1857.
Ordained a Missionary to Africa, May 29, 1887.
Died at Blantyre, November 10, 1890.

This Tablet is erected
by
The MEMBERS of the CHURCH OF SCOTLAND YOUNG MEN'S GUILD,
in Memory of
the First of their Number laid in a Missionary's Grave.

"TILL HE COME."

VII.
Conclusion.

VII.

CONCLUSION.

THUS they died at their posts,—three good men and true,—and the world is the poorer for their loss; but, though dead, Henderson, Bowie, and Cleland still speak to us. When the Angel of Death had folded his wings, that was a sadly stricken community over which he had passed. Blantyre was left almost a wreck of its former self—"almost a mission skeleton of three lonely house-occupants at the three corners of the place,"—a few brave hearts strained almost to the breaking. Yet they never gave way, and out of their very need came a voice whose appeal reached the heart of the Church at home. It is the day of battle which calls forth the soldier spirit, and we do not wonder that the story of courage, endurance, and death, instead of deterring, should awake a spirit of chivalry and call forth offer after offer to go and occupy the vacant posts. The Church had hardly time to record her sorrow over the fallen, and to thank God for the work they had done, ere she was laying hands of benediction on others going forth to take up the work that had fallen from their hands. Already five new missionaries have gone to join the staff of the Mission, and no better wish could be offered as we bid them "God speed" than that they may catch something of the spirit of those whom they have gone to succeed.

A widespread desire has been expressed that some fitting memorial should be found to cherish the memory of those who, in Blantyre, laid down their lives in the service of Christ, and it is felt that the true memorial must be something which will help to perpetuate their spirit and continue their work. It has, therefore, been proposed that a CLELAND MEMORIAL CHURCH should one day be erected on Mount Milanje,— where Robert Cleland so fearlessly and laboriously laid the foundations of a Christian Mission. In Blantyre, too, there will surely be ere long a BOWIE HOSPITAL— such an hospital as Dr. Bowie longed for—where the loving, patient, skilful care with which he tended his poor black patients may be continued by others, labouring, like him, for Christ's sake. Then on the River Shiré there is to be—and very soon, we hope— a MISSION STEAMER bearing the name of Henry Henderson, which, like the pioneer missionary himself, will in future go down to meet the outgoing mission-party at the coast, and conduct them up the river to their field of labour; only doing it with a speed, health, and comfort unknown in former days. It will also overcome the difficulties in the way of evangelizing those river tribes, whose chiefs and villages are praying us to come to them, but whose home

CONCLUSION. 143

is where the European may not dwell, and whom, therefore, only a Mission Steamer, with a man of the Cleland stamp in charge of it, can effectually reach.

Such monuments are proposed, and doubtless there are many who will count it a privilege to have a share in providing them. Worthy memorials they will be of three such lives, for they will secure the continuance of the work done by those whose names they bear. But, after all, these will be but *tools*, and their worth as memorials will depend on the kind of men who use them. In the little missionary band now holding the field in Central Africa there are to-day as brave hearts and true as any that are gone. But they are sorely in need of help, and they appeal to us for it. The burden is too heavy,—the work is too much,—the possibilities are too great for them to bear alone; and the voice of the living and the memory of the dead alike cry to us,—"Pray ye the Lord of the harvest that He would send forth more labourers into the harvest." There is no field in the world where consecrated men and women are more needed, or in which they can better invest loving service for Jesus' sake. This is the true memorial which the Church must raise to lives like these—men and women cherishing their memory, breathing their spirit, following in their footsteps—to render, through the Church and the Hospital and the Mission Steamer, loving Christ-like service to the poor dark children of Africa. Will the Church at home furnish these? In closing the book which tells the story of those Martyrs of Blantyre, may one venture to wonder whether among those who may read that story there may not be some one who will hear in it a call to self-consecration—some one who, giving himself to God and to Africa, may one day bring to the Mission the watchful care of a Henderson, the heroic devotion and skill of a Bowie, or the consecrated enthusiasm and labour of a Cleland? The Lord grant it in His time!

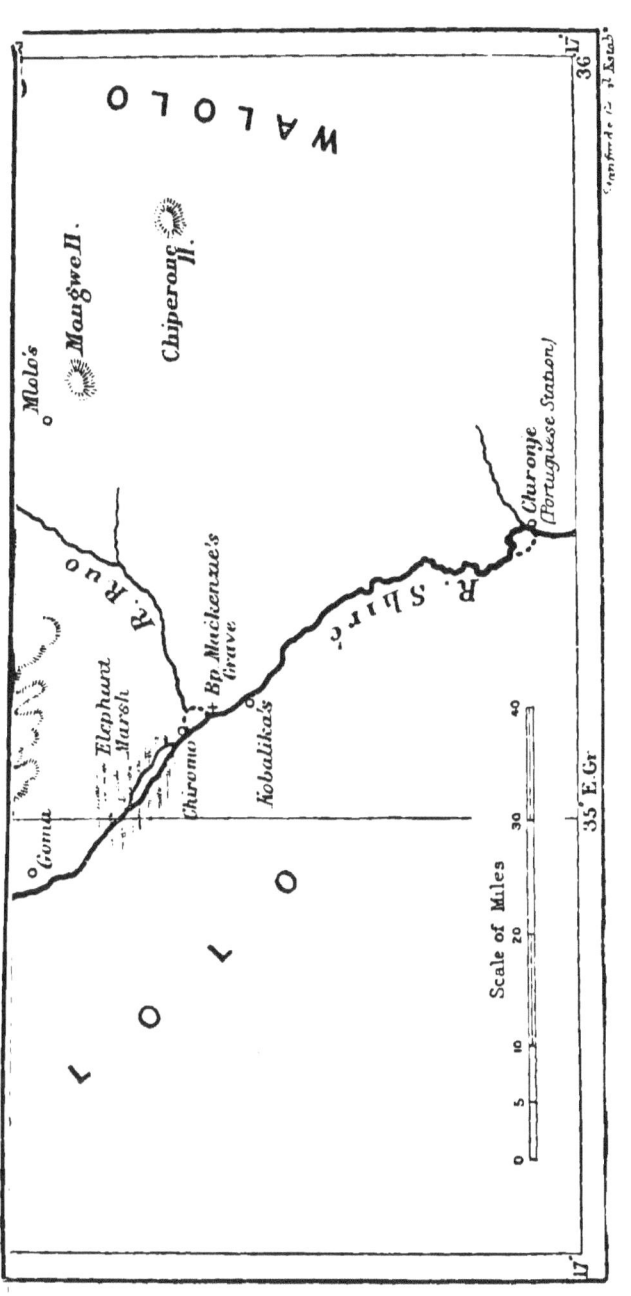

CHART OF THE SHIRÉ HIGHLANDS, SHOWING THE MISSION STATIONS AND SCHOOLS OF THE CHURCH OF SCOTLAND, 1890. BY REV. A. HETHERWICK, F.R.G.S.

APPENDIX.

APPENDIX.

I.

THE CHURCH OF SCOTLAND MISSION TO BRITISH CENTRAL AFRICA.

EUROPEAN STAFF IN 1892.

BLANTYRE (*Founded* 1875).
Rev. D. C. Scott, B.D., F.R.S.G.S. (1881), and Mrs. Scott; John M'Ilwain, Industrial (1884); Miss Janet Beck (1887); Mrs. Fenwick; John A. Smith, Teacher (1888), and Mrs. Smith; Rev. W. A. Scott, M.A., M.B., C.M., (1889); George Adamson, Industrial (1891); James Reid, General Agent (1891); H. D. Herd, Teacher (1891).

DOMASI (*Founded* 1884).
Rev. A. Hetherwick, M.A., F.R.G.S. (1883); R. S. Hynde, Teacher (1888), and Mrs. Hynde; Miss Margaret Christie (1889); Rev. H. E. Scott, L.R.C.P. and S.E. (1890); Miss Euphemia Edie (1891).

CHIRAZULO (*Founded* 1887).
Founded by the late Rev. R. Cleland. At present worked by Native Teachers from Blantyre.

MILANJE (*Founded* 1890.)
Founded by the late Rev. R. Cleland. Rev. Adam Currie, M.A. (1891); George Robertson, L.R.C.P and S.E. (1891).

II.

TRIBUTE PAID TO THE MEMORY OF THE BLANTYRE MISSIONARIES BY THE GENERAL ASSEMBLY OF THE CHURCH OF SCOTLAND.

The Church's sense of the loss sustained by the death of those missionaries is expressed in the following:—

MINUTE of GENERAL ASSEMBLY as to the Deaths of Missionaries at Blantyre.

At Edinburgh, the 1st day of June 1891, Which day the General Assembly of the Church of Scotland being met and constituted, *inter alia*,—The General Assembly having been informed by its Foreign Mission Committee of the death at Blantyre on 10th November of the Rev. Robert Cleland; the death at Blantyre on 13th January of Mrs. Henry Henderson; the death at Blantyre on 17th January of Dr. John Bowie; the death at Quilimane on 12th February of Mr. Henry Henderson,—desires to record in its Minutes a tribute of respect to those greatly lamented missionaries, an extract thereof to be sent to the relatives of the deceased.

Mr. Robert Cleland was born in Coatbridge in 1857, and served an apprenticeship as an engineer. In his twenty-first year he decided to study for the ministry, with the view of becoming a missionary in Africa. He was ordained in St. George's Church, Edinburgh, on 29th May 1887, and sailed from London on 9th June following. During his short career of less than three and a half years in Africa he founded the mission-station of Chirazulo and was pioneer missionary to Mount Milanje. In addition to his own work, he took charge of Domasi Mission for sixteen months, making good roads and bringing in good water, while at the same time labouring with singular consecration as a missionary. He was on a tour of inspection on Mount Milanje when he was seized with the fever from which, five days afterwards, he died at Blantyre.

Mr. John Bowie, M.B., C.M., was the son of an esteemed citizen of Edinburgh, and was a very distinguished student at the University of that city, carrying off the gold medals in Physiology, Natural History, Practice of Medicine, &c. He had entered on a London practice, and was rising into eminence, when he made up his mind to devote his life to mission-work in Africa, joining his brother-in-law, the Rev. D. C. Scott, B.D., at Blantyre. He went out to Africa early in the summer of 1887, accompanied by Mrs. Bowie. His great skill as a physician and surgeon and his true missionary spirit made him a pillar of strength to the African Mission, and his death is deeply deplored alike by Europeans and natives. Always kind and ready to encounter every danger in the path of duty, he died of diphtheria, contracted in an attempt to save the life of his sister's infant son by sucking the tracheotomy tube when the child was dying of that disease.

Mrs. Henry Henderson, born Harriet Bowie, sister of Dr. Bowie and of Mrs. D. C. Scott, was married and went out to Africa not much more than two years ago. Of a bright and happy nature, with a deep under-current of religious life, and as able as she was earnest, she was peculiarly fitted for the duties of a missionary's wife. She also died of diphtheria, after the death of her only child. Before she died, Dr. Bowie, then himself very ill, rose from bed and relieved her sufferings, though he could not save her life, by performing the operation of tracheotomy with all his usual skill.

Mr. Henry Henderson was a son of the late minister of the parish of Kinclaven, and passed through a full Arts course at the University of Edinburgh. He was for some time in Australia, and there a career was opened to him which would probably have led to wealth. But when the Church of Scotland proposed to undertake an African Mission, he volunteered to be pioneer missionary; and to him is due the selection of the comparatively healthy Shiré Highlands, now included in the British protectorate, and forming a stronghold from which the country can be evangelised and civilised. Bereft of wife and child, he set out for Europe, taking charge of Mrs. Bowie and Miss Beck, and reached Quilimane apparently in good health. But there he became ill of fever on 9th January, and died four days afterwards.

Of those good and brave missionaries who have thus died in the mission-field, it can truly be said that there was not a thought of self in any one of them; and by laying down their precious lives for Africa, they have pledged the Church of Scotland to prosecution of their noble enterprise.

The Assembly expresses its deepest sympathy with the widowed mother of Mr. Cleland; with Mrs. Bowie, senior, so sorely bereaved of her children; with the widow and young daughter of Dr. John Bowie; with Mrs. David Clement Scott; and with the other sorrowing relatives, and commends them all to the keeping of Almighty God.

Extracted from the Records of the General Assembly of the Church of Scotland by me,

WM. MILLIGAN, *C. Eccles. Scot.*

Just Published.

Small Crown 8vo, price 1s.

FOREIGN MISSIONS OF THE PROTESTANT CHURCHES:

THEIR STATE AND PROSPECTS.

By the Rev. J. MURRAY MITCHELL, M.A., LL.D.

"A graphic and succinct account, statistical and otherwise, of the work accomplished by the several Missionary Societies."—*Liverpool Mercury.*

"It is simply astonishing that so clear and comprehensive a *résumé* of the methods and conditions of Missionary Enterprise should be compressed into such small compass. This book should be in the hands of all who are interested in Missions."—*Literary World.*

"A very useful and entertaining little work, giving a general glance at the present condition of the different Pagan religions, and the results of Christian effort. Dr. Mitchell's remarks on Mahommedanism and Hinduism are interesting in the light of recent controversy. The book deserves a warm welcome."—*Rock.*

"Such a book was needed, and Dr. Mitchell has met the need well."—*Methodist Recorder.*

"We trust the book will have the attention it deserves; and that its thoughtful pages may call forth active workers, and interest those who have the means wherewith more workers may be sent into the field."—*Christian.*

LONDON: JAMES NISBET & CO., 21 BERNERS STREET, W.

BOOKS ON HOME AND FOREIGN MISSION AND EVANGELISTIC WORK

PUBLISHED BY

JAMES NISBET & CO.

THE CRISIS OF MISSIONS; or, The Voice Out of the Cloud. By ARTHUR T. PIERSON, D.D. Small crown 8vo, 3s. 6d.

"An outline of the condition, extent, development, and promise of Christian Missions. The special work of Women Missionaries finds a place here, and a vivid picture is drawn of the present position, needs, and prospects of Christian Missions."—*Literary World*.

THE GREAT VALUE AND SUCCESS OF FOREIGN MISSIONS. Proved by Distinguished Witnesses: Being the Testimony of Diplomatic Ministers, Consuls, Naval Officers, and Scientific and other Travellers in Heathen and Mohammedan Countries. Also leading Facts and late Statistics of the Missions. By the Rev. JOHN LIGGINS. With an Introduction by the Rev. ARTHUR T. PIERSON, D.D. Crown 8vo, 3s. 6d.

REPORT OF THE CENTENARY CONFERENCE OF PROTESTANT MISSIONS OF THE WORLD, held in Exeter Hall, from the 9th to the 19th June 1888. Edited by the Rev. JAMES JOHNSTON, Secretary of the Committee of Conference. Two Vols. Crown 8vo, 8s.

A CENTURY OF CHRISTIAN PROGRESS, and its Lessons. By the Rev. JAMES JOHNSTON. Crown 8vo, 3s.

THIRTY-EIGHT YEARS' MISSION LIFE IN JAMAICA: A Brief Sketch of the Rev. WARRAND CARLILE, Missionary at Brownsville. By one of his SONS. Small crown 8vo, 3s. 6d.

SOUTH AFRICA AND ITS MISSION FIELDS. By the Rev. J. E. CARLYLE, late Presbyterian Minister and Chaplain, Natal. Post 8vo, 5s.

THE BIBLE IN THE PACIFIC. By the Rev. A. W. MURRAY, Author of "Eminent Workers," &c. Crown 8vo, 5s.

BRIEF SKETCHES OF C.M.S. MISSIONS: Designed to provide material for Missionary Addresses. By EMILY HEADLAND. With Preface by EUGENE STOCK, Editorial Secretary of the Church Missionary Society. In Three Parts. Crown 8vo, 1s.; in boards, 1s. 6d. each.

THE WHITE FIELDS OF FRANCE: An Account of Mr. M'All's Mission to the Working Men of Paris. By the Rev. HORATIUS BONAR, D.D. Crown 8vo, 3s. 6d.

BY THE SAME AUTHOR.

DOES GOD CARE FOR OUR GREAT CITIES? A Word for the Paris Mission. 18mo, 9d.

THE RESPONSIBILITY OF THE HEATHEN AND THE RESPONSIBILITY OF THE CHURCH. By the Rev. C. F. CHILDE, M.A., Rector of Holbrook, Suffolk. 16mo, 1s.

HINDU WOMEN, with Glimpses into their Life and Zenanas. By Miss H. LLOYD, Editorial Secretary of the Church of England Zenana Missionary Society. Crown 8vo, 2s. 6d.

TWELVE MONTHS IN MADAGASCAR. By the late Rev. J. MULLENS, D.D., formerly Foreign Secretary of the London Missionary Society. With Illustrations. Post 8vo, 7s. 6d.

PREACHING TOURS AND MISSIONARY LABOURS OF GEORGE MULLER, OF BRISTOL. By Mrs. MULLER. With Portrait. Crown 8vo, 3s. 6d.

THE NEW HEBRIDES AND CHRISTIAN MISSIONS. With Notes of the Labour Traffic and Kidnapping; and a Cruise through the Group in the Mission Vessel. By the Rev. ROBERT STEEL, D.D., Sydney, N.S.W., Author of "Doing Good," &c. With Frontispiece and Map of the New Hebrides. Post 8vo 8s. 6d.

THE BRIER AND THE MYRTLE; or, Heathenism and Christianity Illustrated in the History of Mary. By Miss TUCKER. Fcap., 1s.

MISSIONS TO THE WOMEN OF CHINA, in Connection with the Society for Promoting Female Education in the East. Crown 8vo, cloth, 2s.

GOD'S ANSWERS: The Narrative of Miss Annie Macpherson's Work at the Home of Industry, Spitalfields. By Miss LOWE. With Illustrations. Crown 8vo, 3s. 6d.

ADDRESSES TO DISTRICT VISITORS AND SUNDAY-SCHOOL TEACHERS. By FRANCIS PIGOU, D.D., Vicar of Halifax. With a Preface by the Right Rev. the BISHOP of ROCHESTER. Small crown 8vo, 2s.

SEEKING THE LOST: Incidents and Sketches of Christian Work in London. By the Rev. C. J. WHITMORE. Crown 8vo, 3s. 6d.

BY THE SAME AUTHOR.

SEEKING AFTER GOD. 16mo, 1s.

HASTE TO THE RESCUE; or, Work while it is Day. By Mrs. CHARLES WIGHTMAN. Crown 8vo, 1s. 6d.

BY THE SAME AUTHOR.

ANNALS OF THE RESCUED. With a Preface by the Rev. C. E. L. WIGHTMAN. Crown 8vo, 3s. 6d.

ARREST THE DESTROYER'S MARCH. Crown 8vo, 3s. 6d.

RAGGED HOMES, AND HOW TO MEND THEM. By Mrs. BAYLY, Author of "The Story of our English Bible," &c. Crown 8vo, 1s. 6d.

"We scarcely know which to praise most highly, the matter or the manner of this work. The author's style is as attractive as her subject. Mrs. Bayly has wrought with an artist's eye and spirit."—*Daily News.*

WORKERS AT HOME. By Mrs. WIGLEY, Author of "Our Home Work." Crown 8vo, 5s.

Separately, as follows, 1s. each.

THOUGHTS FOR MOTHERS.

THOUGHTS FOR CHILDREN.

THOUGHTS FOR SERVANTS.

THOUGHTS FOR TEACHERS.

THOUGHTS FOR YOUNG WOMEN IN BUSINESS.

THE MISSING LINK; or, Bible-Women in the Homes of the London Poor. By L. N. R., Author of "The Book and its Story." Crown 8vo, 3s. 6d. A Cheaper Edition, 1s. 6d.

BY THE SAME AUTHOR.

NURSES FOR THE NEEDY; or, The Bible-Women Nurses in the Homes of the London Poor. Crown 8vo, 3s. 6d.

OUR COFFEE-ROOM. By Lady HOPE of Carriden. With Preface by Lieut.-General Sir ARTHUR COTTON, R.E., K.C.S.I. Crown 8vo, 3s. 6d.

BY THE SAME AUTHOR.

MORE ABOUT "OUR COFFEE-ROOM." Crown 8vo, 3s. 6d.

The late Earl CAIRNS said—"It was one of the most interesting stories he had ever had the pleasure of reading, and showed what a lady could do when she undertook and rightly worked a design and place of that kind with such objects."

LINES OF LIGHT ON A DARK BACKGROUND. Crown 8vo, 3s. 6d.

"Calculated to be of signal service to all who are labouring in the temperance cause."—*Churchman's Magazine*.

LIFE IN HOSPITAL. By a Sister. 16mo, 1s.

"This little book should be read by all. It is far too brief; that is its one fault."—*London Quarterly Review.*

THE HAPPY HOME. By James Hamilton, D.D. New Edition. With Illustrations. 18mo, 1s. 6d.

Contents:—The Friend of the People—The Ship of Neaver—A Bunch in the Hand and More in the Bush—The Oasis—The Fireside—Day Dreaming—Fire Flies—The Faithful Tenant—The True Disciple.

COMFORT: A Book for the Cottage. By Jane Besemeres. 16mo, 1s.

HINTS TO HOSPITAL AND SICK-ROOM VISITORS. By Mrs. Colin G. Campbell. Crown 8vo, 1s. 6d.

BRIGHT GLIMPSES FOR MOTHERS' MEETINGS. By a Mother. With a Preface by the Rev. Thomas Vores, late Vicar of St. Mary's, Hastings. Crown 8vo, 1s. 6d.

By the same Author.

PRAYERS FOR MOTHERS' MEETINGS. 16mo, 6d.; paper cover, 3d.

HOME THOUGHTS FOR MOTHERS AND MOTHERS' MEETINGS. By the Author of "Sick-bed Vows, and How to Keep Them." Crown 8vo, 1s. 6d.

TOILING IN ROWING: Half-Hours of Earnest Converse with my Hard-working Friends. By One who Knows and Loves Them. Second Edition.

NELLIE: A Story of Prison Life. By Mrs. Meredith. Crown 8vo, 1s. 6d.

By the same Author.

A BOOK ABOUT CRIMINALS. Crown 8vo, 3s. 6d.

REMARKABLE ANSWERS TO PRAYER. By JOHN RICHARDSON PHILLIPS, formerly Country Association Agent for the London City Mission. Crown 8vo, 3s. 6d.

BY THE SAME AUTHOR.

REMARKABLE PROVIDENCES AND PROOFS OF A DIVINE REVELATION. With Thoughts, Facts, and Anecdotes Calculated to Strengthen Faith. Fifth Edition. With Illustrations. Crown 8vo, 3s. 6d.

REMARKABLE CASES OF CONVERSION AND OTHER EXPERIENCES, showing the Value of Faith in the Faithful Promiser. Crown 8vo, 3s. 6d.

PLEASANT FRUITS; or, Records of the Cottage and the Class. By MARIA V. G. HAVERGAL. Seventh Edition. Crown 8vo, 2s. 6d.

TERSE TALKS ON TIMELY TOPICS. By HENRY VARLEY. Crown 8vo, 3s. 6d.

ILLUSTRATIVE SCRIPTURE READINGS: A Manual for Visitation and Devotion. By the Rev. T. E. COZENS COOKE. 16mo, 2s.; roan, 3s.

GEMS FROM THE BIBLE: Being Selections Convenient for Reading to the Sick and Aged. Crown 8vo, 3s. 6d.

COTTAGE READINGS IN THE BOOK OF EXODUS. Crown 8vo, 5s.

THE CHRISTIAN VISITOR'S TEXT-BOOK. By the Rev. CHARLES NEIL, M.A. Crown 8vo, 2s.

THE VISITOR'S BOOK OF TEXTS; or, The Word brought Nigh to the Sick and Sorrowful. By A. A. BONAR, D.D. Sixth Edition. Crown 8vo, 3s. 6d.

INVITATIONS. By Lady HOPE of Carriden. 16mo, 1s. 6d. In a packet, 16mo, 1s.; separately, 2d. each.

AWAKENING AND INVITING CALLS. Tracts. By the Very Rev. HENRY LAW, M.A., late Dean of Gloucester. 16mo, 6d.

THE SINNER'S FRIEND. By J. V. HALL. 32mo, 1d., 2d., and 3d. Large type, 6d. paper cover; 1s. cloth limp; 1s. 6d. cloth gilt.

OF WHAT DOES IT CONSIST? or, The Elements of Saving Truth in "A Basket of Fragments and Crumbs." By Lieutenant-Colonel M. J. ROWLANDSON. 16mo, 1s. 6d.

COME TO JESUS. By NEWMAN HALL, LL.B. 32mo, 1d., 2d., and 6d. 16mo, 1s. cloth; 1s. 6d. cloth gilt. Also an Edition in 8vo, large type, 1s. 6d.; 1s. paper cover.

BY THE SAME AUTHOR.

FOLLOW JESUS. A Sequel to "Come to Jesus." 32mo, 3d.

MY FRIENDS. 32mo, 4d.

"IT IS I;" or, The Voice of Jesus in the Storm. 16mo, 6d. Cloth gilt, 1s.

THE BLOOD OF JESUS. A Book for Anxious Inquirers. By the Rev. WILLIAM REID. 16mo, 6d. sewed; 8d. cloth limp; 1s. cloth boards. Large type, 1s. Paper cover, 1s. 6d.

BY THE SAME AUTHOR.

THE SPIRIT OF JESUS. 16mo, 9d. Paper Cover, 6d.

EARTH'S EXPEDIENTS AND HEAVEN'S GOSPEL. 16mo, 6d.

MUSICAL LEAFLETS. In Packets, 1s.

LIGHT FOR THE DARK; or, Bible Words for Inquirers. Crown 8vo, 2s. 6d.

ENGLISH HEARTS AND ENGLISH HANDS; or, The
Railway and the Trenches. By Miss MARSH. Crown 8vo, 5s.
Cheaper Edition, 2s.

The *Times*, referring to Miss Marsh's books, has said—"The Memorials of Vicars and these memorials of the Crystal Palace navvies are books of precisely the same type. We recognise in them an honesty of purpose, a purity of heart, and a warmth of human affection, combined with a religious faith, that are very beautiful."

BY THE SAME AUTHOR.

WHAT MIGHT HAVE BEEN: A True Story. 1s.

FROM DARK TO DAWN; or, The Story of Warwick
Roland. 2d. sewed; 4d. limp cloth; 6d. gilt edges.

DREAMLIGHT FROM HEAVEN AND HEAVENLY
REALITIES. 16mo, 6d.

MIDNIGHT CHIMES; or, The Voice of Hope. 1d.

DEATH AND LIFE: Records of the Cholera Wards in the
London Hospital. 6d.; paper cover, 3d.

BRAVE, KIND, AND HAPPY. Words of Hearty Friendship to the Working Men of England. 1d.

LIGHT FOR THE LINE; or, The Story of Thomas Ward,
a Railway Workman. 6d.; paper cover, 4d.

THE GOLDEN CHAIN. 1s. 6d; paper cover, 6d.

THE RIFT IN THE CLOUDS. 1s.

CROSSING THE RIVER. 1s.

SHINING LIGHT. 1s.

THE RACE AND THE PRIZE. 1d.

READY. 1d.

HEROES OF THE MINE. 9d.

THE DAY DAWN. 1d.

THE HAVEN AND THE HOME. 6d.; paper cover, 3d.

WORDS OF HEARTY FRIENDSHIP TO SOLDIERS,
SAILORS, AND WORKING MEN, containing—Death and Life; Light for the Line; The Haven and the Home; Brave, Kind, and Happy; The Race and the Prize; Ready; Day Dawn; Midnight Chimes. In Packets, price 1s.

ROCK versus SAND;

Or, The Foundations of the Christian Faith.

By J. MONRO GIBSON, D.D.

Third Edition. Crown 8vo, 1s. 6d.

"This volume displays rare skill and originality in its structure and composition. We commend the book most heartily, as one in every way serviceable to the cause of truth."—*Christian.*

"This book, which literally bristles with argumentative weapons of the finest temper, will be regarded as a boon by those who have not the time or opportunity to enter largely into these momentous questions, but who wish to be able to answer the fashionable objections against the Bible and its teachings."—*Methodist Recorder.*

ALIKE AND PERFECT;

Or, God's Three Revelations.

By the Rev. C. A. WILLIAMS.

Crown 8vo, 3s. 6d.

"The idea of the book is familiar, but the treatment has all the freshness, crispness of speech, fertility of illustration, and directness of purpose that characterise much of the best American literature. In harmonising God's revelation of Himself in the spheres of Creation, Providence, and the Divine Word, the author avoids much of the argumentation we are accustomed to on this theme, and leads us into tracts of thought at once suggestive and impressive."—*Presbyterian Magazine.*

"This valuable treatise will prove attractive alike in its descriptions of natural scenery, in its references to the finger of God in history, and in its clear enunciation of the Divine method for fallen man's restoration."—*Record.*

THE HEBREW FEASTS

IN RELATION TO RECENT CRITICAL HYPOTHESES REGARDING THE PENTATEUCH.

By the Rev. W. H. GREEN, D.D.

Crown 8vo, 5s.

"This volume is directed especially against the destructive criticism of Reuss, Wellhausen, and Kuenen upon the date, unity, and authenticity of the Pentateuch. Dr. Green brings ability, learning, and critical faculty to the task he has undertaken, and has presented a strong case for the Conservative view."—*Church Times.*

"Lectures of remarkable ability, written in excellent taste and style. We most cordially recommend them to all interested in Biblical criticism. Dr. Green sends a fresh blast of common sense through the 'wood of error,' and it is really marvellous how before it the air clears and phantoms disappear."
—*Literary Churchman.*

LONDON: JAMES NISBET & CO., 21 BERNERS STREET, W.

www.ingramcontent.com/pod-product-compliance
Lightning Source LLC
Chambersburg PA
CBHW020301170426
43202CB00008B/452